PR BIBLE

FOR

COMMUNITY
THEATRES

THE

PR BIBLE

FOR

COMMUNITY
THEATRES

CHRIS MACKOWSKI

3 1336 06111 5011

HEINEMANN
PORTSMOUTH, NH

HEINEMANN
A division of Reed Elsevier Inc.
361 Hanover Street
Portsmouth, NH 03801–3912
www.heinemanndrama.com

Offices and agents throughout the world

Library of Congress Cataloging-in-Publication Data
Mackowski, Chris.
The PR bible for community theatres / Chris Mackowski.
    p.   cm.
ISBN 0-325-00440-4 (alk. paper)
    1. Community theater—Handbooks, manuals, etc.   2. Publicity—
Handbooks, manuals, etc.   I. Title: Public relations bible for
community theatres.   II. Title.

PN2267 .M34   2002
792'.022—dc21   2002003541

Editor: Lisa A. Barnett
Production editor: Sonja S. Chapman
Cover design: Darci Mehall, Aureo Design
Manufacturing: Steve Bernier
Typesetter: TechBooks

Printed in the United States of America on acid-free paper
06 05 04 03 02   DA   1 2 3 4 5

ontents

Acknowledgments   vii

Introduction   ix

1   Everything You Ever Needed to Know About PR (Crammed into One Chapter)   1

2   Who's Out There and What Do They Think of You? (How Research Can Help You Identify and Evaluate Your Relationships)   8

3   How'd They Know That? (And Why Didn't They Know Something Else?)   12

4   Newspaper Editors Don't Want to Be Your Friends (But They Do Want to Be Hooked)   21

5   Quest for the Holy Grail (The Magazine Feature)   38

6   Radio Daze   44

7   TV or Not TV? That Is the Question   57

8   The World Wide Whatsit? (And Why It's So Important)   65

9   You've Got the Look (And Everything You Do Should, Too)   78

10   Your Season Brochure Sets the Tone   86

11   Your Newsletter Is Your Best Friend   97

12   The Three Ps   110

13   A Few Words About Printing   121

14 Picture This   128

15 Bright Ideas   137

16 Getting Your Act Together: Drafting Your PR
   and Marketing Plan   151

   Appendix   164

Acknowledgments

The thing I love most about community theatre is the sense of community we all share. It *is* the arts, after all, and if we don't hang together . . . well, *you* know.

It's sometimes tough to keep our theatre magic alive when so many people act as if the arts don't matter. But the arts *do* matter. They enrich our lives. They give us new perspectives. They make us better people. In the course of writing this book, I found it affirming to interact with so many people who share that vision.

Literally hundreds of community theatres contributed their stories and strategies to me. Individuals from more than a dozen other theatres took time to sit and chat with me over coffee, give me tours of their theatres, trade email, or shoot the breeze on the telephone. Their wisdom and experience is sprinkled liberally through these pages, and I thank them all.

In particular, I'd like to thank Lucy Rioux of Monmouth Community Players in Monmouth, Maine; Rod McCullough and Patricia Fackler of the Fulton Opera House in Lancaster, Pennsylvania; Tony Allegretti of Theatre Jacksonville in Jacksonville, Florida; Sam Kuba of Theatre Harrisburg in Harrisburg, Pennsylvania; Kathy Morrison of the Theatre of Dare in Nag's Head, North Carolina; Steve Helsel of Altoona Community Theatre in Altoona, Pennsylvania; Mary Jean Morrison of the Puget Sound Musical Theatre in Des Moines, Washington; "Doc" Carale Manning-Hill of Gem Theatre in Claude, Texas; and Erica "The Theatre Zombie" Carl of the Little Theatre of Mechanicsburg in Mechanicsburg, Pennsylvania.

I owe a special thanks to Olean Community Theatre in Olean, New York, and Bradford Little Theatre in Bradford, Pennsylvania. Both companies have been extremely gracious to me over the years, allowing me to practice my professional craft and express my artistic vision.

From the media side of the fence, a number of professionals—
many of them my friends—offered their expertise. I thank them all
for sharing their wisdom (which, in the long run, will make their jobs
easier!). Thanks especially to Glenn Melvin for his assistance with
the photography in this book, and to Rachel Rogers, who's the best
designer I've ever worked with. Thanks, too, to Dan Wintermantel
for his groovy artwork.

I would also like to thank Mark Van Tilburg, a true friend
and mentor; Tim Ziakus; Mike Hill of St. Bonaventure's Quick Arts
Center; and Lee Coppola and the faculty and staff of the Russell J.
Jandoli School of Journalism and Mass Communication at
St. Bonaventure University in Allegany, New York, with special thanks
to Brother Basil Valente, O.F.M., and Patrick Vecchio.

I can't imagine I could've ended up with friendlier editors anywhere than Lisa Barnett and Sonja Chapman. All the editors I've
ever known were newspaper editors, and I'm not sure anyone would
characterize them as a breed of "warm and fuzzy" people. Lisa and
Sonja give me hope that editors *do* have souls.

Of course, any true community begins at home. My wife, Heidi,
and my children, Stephanie and Jackson, showed tremendous patience with me as I wrote this book. Heidi, in particular, has waited
for years for all this writing to pay off, so it's gratifying to finally have
a book to dedicate to her.

And now, if you'll excuse me, I owe my daughter a much-delayed
game of air hockey . . .

ntroduction

I am a Gemini.

I tell you that only because it will help you understand how and why I put this book together. Otherwise, it's safe to assume my astrological sign is of no use or interest to you whatsoever. I, myself, don't even believe in astrology, although I have to remind myself once in a while that there must be *something* to it. After all, I am about as "split personality" as Geminis come.

Half of me is a pragmatic, nuts-and-bolts, details kind of guy. That part has allowed me to have a career as an award-winning journalist, a PR guy, and now a professor of public relations and mass communication.

But then there's that *other* half of me. That half of me that's a Theatre Person. That other half is the creative part that sits at the computer writing madly until three A.M. . . . the part that likes to read plays as much as watch them . . . the part that serves as artistic director for our local community theatre.

I've reconciled my two halves, at least in part, by writing this book. My goal is to give you a lot of specific "how-to" advice, gained from hard-earned personal experience in the trenches of community theatre and hard-earned professional experience in the trenches of a PR office that promoted a lot of arts events. I know firsthand the unique challenges community theatres deal with because I have dealt with them myself.

Throughout the book, I'll keep coming back to a few overarching principles that should guide your PR efforts. I'll quickly spell them out for you now so you can start looking for them. That way, should something dreadful happen—like the rest of this book spontaneously combusts or gets eaten by your dog or whatever—you'll at least have had a preview:

- *Have a plan.* Have a plan for each show you do, but more importantly, have an overall plan to promote your theatre company. This is the number one reason public relations should be a function of your board or a single paid staff person, and not done on a show-by-show basis.
- *Know your audience.* Your audience should drive every single thing you, as a theatre company, do. Therefore, know your audience well.
- *Make things as easy as possible for editors.* You'll hear me stress this over and over and over... and still, I won't be able to stress it enough.
- *Find yourself a good writer.* A good writer working with your theatre company is just as crucial, if not more so, as a good stage manager in the wings or sound person at the mixing board during a show. Good writing is the secret to effective PR.

Being the pragmatic guy that half of me is, I'm going to give you lots of nuts-and-bolts advice because that's what you want and what your company needs. But rather than just tell you what to do and how to do it, I'll also sprinkle in a lot of "why." You'll be better served, I think, if you have an understanding of and appreciation for why I offer the advice I do, because that will allow you to better adapt my advice to your company's specific circumstances. To that end, I'll share a little PR and mass communication theory, some personal experiences from other community theatre people, and tips from professionals in the media.

I also realize your time, personnel, and resources are all at a premium, and the procedures and ideas presented here take that into account. If your community theatre is anything like the ones I've worked with, you don't have the luxuries professional theatres have, with their big payrolls of paid staff members who handle marketing and public relations and leave the Theatre People blissfully alone to do their creative thing. Instead, you have a core of devoted, hard-working volunteers and maybe an overworked, underpaid staff person or two. Everyone wears a multitude of hats, and that's not even counting the jobs and families y'all have in the real world.

One of your company's devoted, hard-working volunteers—probably *you*, since you're the one reading this book—has agreed to wear the hat of PR Person. It may or may not be an area in which you have any sort of expertise, but either way, this book will help you.

And now that you're living a double life, you can be an official Honorary Gemini. Welcome to the club!

Everything You Ever Needed to Know About PR ((rammed into One Chapter)

or Theatre People, public relations is a necessary evil. After all, it doesn't directly relate to the productions we create. It isn't something we can do onstage or behind the scenes. We don't compose it in the pit, nor do we build it in the scene shop. But certainly our *audience* does directly relate to our productions. A play, after all, does not fulfill itself as a piece of theatre until it's performed in front of, and absorbed by, an audience.

YOU *NEED* AN AUDIENCE, a statement so obvious I probably don't need to say it, let alone put it in capital letters. But I say it to remind you why the "necessary evil" is so necessary: An audience won't come to your show if it doesn't know your show is happening.

And how is it that an audience knows your show is happening? (Said the pincushion to the pin, "I get your point.")

While the primary function of PR is to reach out to people, the process of creating PR is generally a solitary endeavor. You don't sit at a computer and write press releases by committee. In fact, writing and theatre are at opposite ends of the creative spectrum, because theatre is inherently social and writing is necessarily solitary. As a result, you may slave away in the solitude of your home or office, working on publicity for a show, and some people in your company will still think the throngs of audience members who come to the show have done so miraculously (or, worse yet, because *they* were in it ... you know the type). So, I'd better warn you right off the bat: PR can sometimes be a thankless job.

However, it's also a job that can be immensely satisfying. And the more you do it, as with anything else, the easier it gets and the better at it *you* get.

What *Is* PR, Anyway?

For starters, it might be helpful to identify what exactly we mean by *public relations* and what that entails.

"Public" Information

First, let's define *public*. Any group of people with whom your theatre interacts makes up a public. That might seem pretty evident, but I could give you a list three pages long, and some of the groups on that list might surprise you. Let me give you just a few:

- your audience (season ticket holders, the Friday night crowd, the Sunday matinee crowd, first-time attendees, regular attendees who don't subscribe, subscribers who seldom come, family members of show participants, people who like musicals, people who don't like musicals, etc.)
- people within your company (board of directors members, volunteers, directors, actors, technicians, musicians, playwrights, committee members, etc.)
- donors (major corporations, small businesses, individuals, people within your company, etc.)
- schools (administrators, English teachers, music teachers, students, musicians, drama club members, choir members, etc.)
- media outlets (newspapers, radio stations, cable TV networks, "the message channel," movie theatres, etc.)
- professional organizations (The American Association of Community Theatres, your state theatre association, regional arts groups, other community theatres, the Dramatists Guild, etc.)

Many of these publics overlap, and individuals may fall into more than one category. A broad, general message may reach many or even most of them, but *specifically targeted messages* will reach more of them more effectively. One of the things this book will do is help you identify potential publics and come up with ways to best target them in your PR.

Because these publics overlap and interrelate, we can look at public relations as our relationships with our publics, their relationships with us, and their relationships with each other. In other words, public relations is *not* a one-way or even a two-way street; it's the Public Works Department's city street map. If you know what the map looks like, you'll have an easier time getting your message everywhere it needs to be.

Functions of PR

When people think of public relations, they think of writing press releases. While that is certainly part of the job, there's a whole lot more. Knowing the different functions of public relations can give you a better idea of the potential avenues for getting out your message. Let's take a look at a quick list:

- writing and submitting press releases
- writing and submitting feature stories
- writing and submitting calendar listings
- serving as contact person for the media
- coordinating photography
- managing the webpage
- overseeing the design and printing of programs
- overseeing the design and printing of posters
- overseeing the distribution of posters
- overseeing the writing, design, and printing of brochures
- overseeing the distribution of brochures
- overseeing the writing, design, and printing of newsletters
- overseeing the distribution of newsletters
- overseeing the writing, design, and printing of annual reports
- overseeing the distribution of annual reports
- creating displays
- coordinating special publicity events and appearances
- compiling and distributing information kits for civic leaders, teachers, and major donors
- contacting schools about productions

- developing a public relations/advertising plan
- scheduling advertisements

We can categorize these various functions into five groups: media relations, civic relations (a term I'll use to encompass government, civic groups, and teachers), donor relations, advertising, and publications.

I should point out that advertising and public relations are two separate things. Although closely related to public relations, advertising is the distribution of a message intended specifically to stimulate sales—in your case, ticket sales. There is such a thing as public relations advertising, which is advertising intended to enhance the image or change the public's perception of your theatre. But in reality, on the community theatre level—particularly with small theatres—public relations and advertising functions are all generally handled by the same person or committee, so for practical purposes, we'll talk about them together.

Now that we know what a PR person does, let's talk about some of the basic principles of public relations.

The Big Three

Anything you say to your publics, ranging from audition announcements to thank-you notes, is a message. But before you craft any message, it's important to consider who the *audience* for the message is, what the *purpose* of that message is, and what your company's and audience's *values* are. I call these The Big Three.

Audience

Simply put, the audience is the group of people who will hear the message. On the surface, that notion seems fairly obvious, but there's a hidden factor involved when it comes to public relations, and that hidden factor can make you or break you.

Most messages you send out will be geared to the general public, right? But how does the public get those messages? In most cases, it's via the media—the newspaper, the radio, the local TV station, etc. And who decides what goes in the paper or over the air? Reporters and editors. *They are an audience.* An important one, too. As David Brinkley once said, "The news is what I say it is."

Think about the implications of that for a minute. If your message doesn't seem like news to a reporter or editor, she isn't going to pass it along to the general public. (That's the first of many reasons you need to make things as easy as possible for editors.) We'll talk more about hooking editors in Chapter 4.

When you consider other groups of people who'll hear your message, it's easy to fall into the trap of thinking in broad terms: the general public, our season ticket holders, people who read *The Hometown Times*, etc. This is an easy but costly mistake. You need to think specific.

For instance, your season ticket holders are made up of a number of subgroups: the Friday night crowd, the Sunday matinee crowd, subscribers who seldom attend, people who like musicals, people who don't like musicals, etc.

What makes each subgroup different? What characteristics do members of each subgroup share?

By identifying your specific audiences and the specific characteristics of each, you can begin to better hone your message. When you do, you not only save resources, you stand a better chance of appealing to your target audience. Some examples:

- A message intended for the general public should be crafted differently than a message intended for season ticket holders.
- A drama intended for mature audiences, something like *A Streetcar Named Desire,* will necessitate a different kind of message than a children's play like *Aesop's Fables.*
- If your audience is typically a younger crowd, your message should be hipper and flashier than a message crafted for an audience made up primarily of senior citizens.
- The number of women typically in your audience will make the difference between referring to *Steel Magnolias* as "a touching drama of family and friendship" or "a chick play."

So, always keep in mind: Who do you want this message to reach?

Purpose

Once you figure out who you want to target, you need to decide why you're targeting them. What is the purpose of the message? Is it to

- Inform? ("Opening this weekend, *The Foreigner* ... ")
- Persuade? (*"Newsday's* Linda Winer called *The Real Thing,* winner of three Tony Awards, including Best Play, 'One of the most gloriously articulate love stories that modern theatre knows enough to cherish.' ")
- Provoke action? ("Get your tickets now at these outlets...")

In PR terms, we call these informational, attitudinal, and behavioral objectives, but there's not going to be a quiz, so you don't need to worry about the labels. What you do need to be conscious of are the functions:

- You want to let people know the details of an upcoming show. (*informational*)
- You want them to come to the show. (*behavioral*)
- You want people to support your theatre and its place in the community. (*attitudinal,* although, of course, goodwill can be parlayed into dollar signs!)

Values

The last component of The Big Three is values. The notion of values goes back to your theatre company's mission statement. Why does your company exist? If it's strictly for entertainment, your messages are going to have a slant different from those of a theatre company whose major focus is on education or on experimental work.

For example, if your mission is to fill as many seats in your theatre as possible, you might call Samuel Beckett's *Waiting for Godot* "a modern classic that has influenced a generation of playwrights." You'd probably leave out any mention of the Theatre of the Absurd, and you would definitely leave out anything that suggests the play challenges an audience on several levels. Those types of things aren't big selling points to a mass audience. On the other hand, if your mission is to expose your community to new types of theatrical experiences, then you'd emphasize the unconventional nature of the play, perhaps calling it "an off-beat tale of waiting... and waiting... and waiting...."

You also need to understand your audience's values. Kristine Thatcher's *Emma's Child* speaks to issues that resonate with church going audiences, but some of the play's language would offend many of those same people. Often, the audience's values are taken into account when you select your line-up of shows for the season, but they also need to be considered when deciding how to publicize those shows.

There's also a third element that relates to values. What are *your* values as a public relations person? If they don't correspond to the company's or the audience's (or even a particular play's) values, you could find yourself in the uncomfortable position of having to promote a play that you don't believe in. I won't say that it can't be done, because it can, but it's something you may want to discuss with the board of directors if you feel strongly enough about it. An honest, straightforward conversation will usually lead to a workable compromise for everyone and save you a lot of grief down the road.

We'll see how to put The Big Three into practice when we pull everything together in Chapter 16.

Word

Finally, let me stress one important and often-overlooked fact: *Word of mouth can be the single most important vehicle for spreading news about a show.*

Do not underestimate its power. Word of mouth is cheap, it's interpersonal, and it has direct appeal. You need to talk up the theatre, and the board needs to talk up the theatre. Cast and crew members, in particular, need to talk up their shows. If you're a cast member, it may feel self-serving to tell everyone you know that you're going to be in a play in two weeks ... but get over it. If you're not excited about the show, why would anyone else be?

Do whatever you can to encourage word of mouth.

Things to Think About

- What PR functions does your theatre company currently do?
- Who is your primary audience?
- Who are your secondary audiences?
- Why do you want to reach your audiences?
- What are your company's values?

Who's Out There and What Do They Think of You? (How Research Can Help You Identify and Evaluate Your Relationships)

During his reelection campaign in 1992, George H. W. Bush fielded a question from a woman at a town-hall style debate. "Mister President," the woman asked, "do you know how much a loaf of bread costs?"

The question stunned him. He didn't know the answer.

As you may recall, Bush lost the election. Arguably the most powerful man in the world, brought down by a loaf of bread.

Did it come as a surprise to me? No. Why? Because that loaf of bread proved an important point: President Bush did not know his audience.

Knowing your audience is the single most important part of successful public relations. If you don't know your public, how can you relate to them?

Who Is Your Audience?

Now, when I say "Know your audience," I don't mean on a personal level. I'm talking on a demographic level (although knowing audience members personally is a good idea, too—the more personal the connection they have with your theatre, the more likely it is that they will keep coming back).

This gets tricky. Finding out about your audience involves a highly complicated, intricate, and technical science, combined with the finesse and intuition of a great art: You ask them.

It's not rocket science. Distribute a survey at your shows. Send one via direct mail, and to increase your response rate, include a self-addressed, stamped envelope. Call your patron list (if you tell patrons you're not calling for money, you may shock them into answering all your questions). Have someone with a clipboard stand next to the refreshment counter at intermission.

You can dangle a carrot in front of people in exchange for their cooperation. People who fill out the survey qualify to win a season ticket for next year, or a T-shirt, or a weekend trip to see Broadway shows. Of course, getting names and addresses from surveys is also a good way to bolster your mailing list.

Some people might feel awkward about answering questions if their name is on the survey, so you can always opt for an anonymous survey. If you do, make sure you at least ask for zip codes so you can sort information geographically. If you know where your audience is coming from, you know where to focus your PR activities.

Aside from location, the survey should also ask about such things as age, gender, education level, and income level (some people are uncomfortable answering income questions, so you might make those optional).

You may also find it helpful to know the racial mix of your audience. Critics may say that's not a politically correct thing to ask about, but if diversity is important to your theatre company from a programming and an audience perspective (and I'll say right up front that it should be), you need to gather data that tells you how diverse an audience you're reaching—or need to reach.

Answers to these questions will help you build a set of demographic profiles for your audience. Get specific: Don't just ask "male or female." You should be able to tell, for instance, what percentage of your audience is made up of women aged thirty-five to fifty who have at least a bachelor's degree.

Another section of the survey should ask about theatregoing preferences. This will give you some data you can draw conclusions from. Some questions you might ask:

- Are you a season ticket holder?
- What day do you usually attend?
- Do you prefer matinees or evening performances?
- Rate your order of preference: musicals, comedies, murder mysteries, dramas. For any of those questions, you can tack on a "Why?" to get more detailed information.

With all that info at your fingertips, you can get a clearer picture of who's coming to your theatre, when. You can then use that information to drive your public relations efforts.

You can also use surveys to get a general idea of what your audience thinks of your theatre. What keeps them coming back? Or prevents them from coming back? What do you do that makes them happy? What do they expect of you?

Finally, you can ask respondents which media outlets they read, listen to, and watch and which forms of publicity they notice. *Knowing which forms of publicity they notice is crucial.*

You may find out that fewer people read the local Sunday arts section in the paper than you thought. You may discover that people are confusing your ads with the ads of another arts group, or that large numbers of people are listening to radio stations you never would've guessed. Prepare to have some of your "conventional wisdom" debunked and some affirmed.

It's a lot of information to ask, and in some ways it's an imposition on your audience members to ask them to spend time filling out surveys. Explain that the surveys are ultimately for their benefit, and then make it as easy as possible for them to respond. Have a box of golf pencils on hand. Have some extra clipboards. Provide a self-addressed, stamped envelope.

Finally, survey your audience at least every few years. The times, they are a-changin' . . . and so are your audiences. The only way to keep up is to keep asking questions and responding to the answers your audience gives you.

What Do the Media Think of You?

Once you pore over the data you've gathered and you know your audience, you're ready to hit the media. But remember, the media aren't just vehicles for getting the word out. The media make up an important part of your audience because they reach so many other members of your audience.

To get acquainted with the media segment of your audience, you first need to spend some time compiling a list of all the media in your local market—all the daily and weekly newspapers, all the AM and FM stations, all the TV affiliates and cable providers, all the magazines or weekly 'zines, and all the community-oriented websites.

Then, talk to folks at each media outlet to find out what they know about your theatre company and what they think of it. If you do it right, it'll be time-intensive, but the effort will be worthwhile. A face-to-face or telephone conversation helps establish or reinforce a relationship between you and the media outlets that will pay dividends down the road.

That's why a survey won't cut it when it comes to learning about your media audience: It's too impersonal. Besides, media folks just don't have the time to fill out surveys, even if a personal chat ends up taking more time than a survey would have.

Not only is it important to know what the media think of you, it's also important to know how the media work and how people—your potential audience members—use the media. And that's what we'll look at in Chapter 3.

Things to Think About

- What's the best way for you to survey your audience?
- Aside from the questions I suggested, what sort of information, specific to your situation, would be appropriate to ask on an audience survey?
- What sort of demographic profiles can you come up with from your surveys?
- What are the media outlets in your local market?
- What do the media outlets think of your theatre?

3 How'd They Know That? (And Why Didn't They Know Something Else?)

When we think of "the media," what comes to mind? Usually we use that term in a negative context: "The media" is responsible. "The media" likes to dig for dirt. "The media" shows too much violence. The media makes an easy scapegoat.

But in reality, the media plays an integral part in our lives. We read the paper in the morning before going to work. We listen to the radio during our commute, and many of us have the radio on at our place of business. On our lunch hour, we might spend time surfing the Web while we eat a sandwich. We check the mail when we get home—hey, there's one of the magazines we subscribe to—and then watch the evening news on TV. We probably watch a few prime-time sitcoms, too. Then we head up to bed and maybe listen to a CD as we drift off to sleep. And let's not forget to turn on that alarm, which is set to have our favorite radio station wake us up.

Any of that sound familiar? Media inundate us with messages all day long, and many people build those interactions into their daily routines. We call those interactions "media-induced rituals," and advertisers and public relations people learned long ago how to take advantage of them. *You* need to take advantage of them, too.

Basically, you have two types of media at your disposal: controlled and uncontrolled.

Controlled Media

Controlled media let you control the way your message is presented. You craft a message, then you send it directly to the audience. Controlled media include

- newsletters
- websites
- brochures
- posters.

For instance, you write the newsletter's stories, so they say what you want them to say. You control the layout, so stories end up where you want them to. You include the pictures you want to include, and you print them as large or as small as you want.

Uncontrolled Media

With uncontrolled media, you depend on someone else (a "gatekeeper," if you want to know more lingo) to get your message out. You lose control of your message and how it's presented. Uncontrolled media include

- newspapers
- radio
- television.

You might have wondered why anyone would use an uncontrolled form of media, but after looking at the examples, I'm sure you see why. Uncontrolled media—(some would say "uncontrollable")—get your message out to a huge audience that you otherwise would not be able to reach.

The success of your message depends on the gatekeepers: reporters, editors, news directors, anchors, announcers, and even the person who lays out and pastes up newspaper pages before they go on to the printing press. Any of them can alter or affect the way your message gets presented to the audience. They decide whether to use the information you give them, how much of it they'll use, and how they'll use it.

For instance, take the information you wrote up for a story in your newsletter. Let's say it sounds something like this:

> The witch-hunt is about to begin at the Tennessee Theatre as the Vogelville Playcrafters present Arthur Miller's classic tale of love and paranoia, *The Crucible*. The excitement gets underway May 31– June 2 at 7:30 P.M. nightly, with a special 2:00 matinee on Sunday, June 3.

Give that same write-up to a newspaper editor, and the editor is likely to change it in some way. The lead might end up looking like this:

> The Vogelville Playcrafters will present Arthur Miller's play *The Crucible* next week.
> Performances will be held at the Tennessee Theatre May 31– June 2 at 7:30 P.M. nightly, with a 2:00 matinee on Sunday, June 3.

Maybe the editor doesn't like the way it was originally written. Maybe the editor doesn't have much space to devote to the piece. Maybe the editor puts the story at the bottom of page four instead of at the top of page one. Those things are all out of your control. In the end, the information does get out to the public, but the way in which the message is presented is affected.

You want to maximize your chances of getting your message out to the public as intact as possible. By understanding the media at your disposal, you can better understand how readers, listeners, and viewers interact with those media. This is where knowing your audience begins to pay off: If you know how the media reach their audiences, you can figure out which media *your* audience is paying attention to, when.

The Mass Media

Each form of mass media, whether controlled or uncontrolled, has attributes that make it unique. A quick rundown of the pros and cons will help (see For More Information, page 20).

Newspapers

Whether daily or weekly, the local newspaper typically has the largest, most experienced newsroom in a community. In a small town, newspaper readership always dominates other media consumption. Newspapers also generate far more money in local advertising revenue than any other form of mass media.

Pros:

- Newspapers contain a broad range of content, which appeals to wide audiences; there's something for everyone in a newspaper, whether it's news, sports, the crossword, "Dear Abby," the funnies, or any of a dozen other regular features.
- Newspapers can go in-depth with their stories.
- You can read newspapers any time and any place. They are portable, too, so if you don't finish an article, you can take the paper with you.
- You can put a newspaper down and come back to it later. You can continue to refer to it over time.
- Newspapers can provide pictures as well as text.
- Newspapers are cheap to buy—fifty cents an issue in many places, maybe two dollars on Sundays.
- Newspapers are readily available and can even be delivered to your door. Many are also available on line.

Cons:

- You need to know how to read.
- If a headline doesn't catch your eye, you probably won't read the story, no matter how well-written it might be.
- The information in a newspaper is dated, even in cities that print multiple editions in a day. The content is not up-to-the-minute.
- Newspaper ink smudges all over your fingertips, which annoys the heck out of some people.

Magazines

Nearly 90 percent of Americans read an average of ten periodicals per month. Since magazines can't compete with newspapers or broadcast media for timeliness, they compensate by going for depth and color.

Magazines also offer amazing specialization aimed at highly specific target audiences.

Pros:
- Content remains timely for months or even years.
- Articles offer in-depth analysis, research, background information, and discussion.
- Magazines can contain full-color pictures, charts, and graphs.
- There's a magazine with a focused topic for nearly any interest.

Cons:
- You have to know how to read.
- It can take awhile to read an entire magazine.
- Magazines aren't a source of timely news.
- Magazines are more expensive than other forms of media.

Radio

Radios outnumber people two to one. The average household has six receivers, and nearly every car has one. Adults listen to an average of twenty-two hours of radio a week, and more adults get their morning news from radio than from any other form of mass media. Communities as small as just a few hundred people have their own radio stations. AM stations tend to be more talk-oriented in their formats, while FM stations tend to be more music-oriented (but there are plenty of exceptions).

Pros:
- Radio is immediate. It's *now.*
- Radio is portable. You can listen to it virtually anywhere.
- Listeners get attached to their favorite radio personalities to the point where they feel like they know the DJ (and in small towns, they usually do!).
- A variety of programming and music formats cater to varying tastes.
- It's free.
- Radio broadcasters can go places television broadcasters can't because there's much less equipment involved. In most cases, a radio broadcaster with nothing more than a cellphone can go live on location.
- You don't need to know how to read to enjoy the content.

Cons:
- You need to own a radio.
- Radio is typically a secondary medium, meaning people listen to the radio while they do something else (drive the car, eat breakfast, take a shower, work, etc.). That makes it challenging to catch and hold a listener's attention.
- Radio has no pictures.
- Because radio is *now,* it's here and then it's gone forever. You can't refer back to something.
- Commercials annoy people.
- Listeners can't choose the specific songs they'll hear, so many will listen to CDs instead of radio.

TV

Arguably the most powerful mass medium, television is also one of the most expensive to generate. That's why you usually find TV stations only in metro areas. Their broadcast signals can carry far into outlying areas, and cable and satellite technology can carry the signals around the world. A typical house has multiple TVs, and the TVs are usually on for a combined average of seven hours a day.

Pros:
- TV provides both pictures and sound.
- It's *now.*
- Specialized cable channels cater to narrow, focused target audiences.
- Broadcast channels are free.
- Watching TV is passive; it doesn't require much brainpower. That can make it a good way to relax and unwind.

Cons:
- Watching TV is passive; it doesn't require much brainpower. That can create couch potatoes.
- You need to own a TV. In some places, you also need to have a cable hookup or a satellite dish.
- Most TV isn't local.
- TV isn't very portable.
- Cable and satellite channels charge a subscription fee and a hookup fee, and sometimes there's even a cost associated with purchasing equipment.

The Web

The Web is a vast global network of interconnected computers that serves as a storehouse of information. Ten years ago, few people envisioned such a thing could exist; today we offhandedly talk about "the information superhighway." Using the Web is a popular way to do research, keep in touch with friends, and shop—particularly among young people. In fact, most Web users typically have a lot of disposable income.

Pros:

- You can find virtually anything on the Web. There's a ton of information.
- You don't have to leave your house to use it.
- It offers text, pictures, movies, and sound.
- It's interactive.

Cons:

- Any yahoo can publish a webpage, which can make it difficult to discern what's credible and what isn't.
- You need a computer, an Internet hookup, and browser software to use the Web. Technical problems can limit access.
- Some websites charge for access or information.
- The Web promotes social isolation. You might feel like you're interacting with other people, but in fact, you are sitting, alone, with a computer. And, it's hard to tell who you're *really* talking to.

Other Forms of Mass Media

Books, movies, and records are also forms of mass media. However, none of them are particularly useful for promoting a community theatre, so for the purposes of this book, we're pretty much going to skip them.

One thing I will mention about books and records, though, is that they can serve as good reference materials for your audience. For instance, if you're doing Lorraine Hansberry's *A Raisin in the Sun,* you might make a copy of the script available at the local library and let the public know it's there in case anyone who's unfamiliar with the show is interested in reading it. The same goes for a CD recording of a musical. Books and CDs give potential audience members the chance to learn more about a show, and if they're interested enough to seek out the script or soundtrack, they'll probably be interested enough to come see your production.

Movie versions of a play can be helpful, but they often hurt more than help. Viewers lock on to a particular image or performance, and anything your company does is unfairly measured against the movie version.

Who Uses What, When

Different groups of people tend to prefer different forms of media:

- Newspaper readers are generally older. Young people, particularly high school and college students, seldom read the paper at all. Readership increases with age. That means if you need high schoolers to audition for a show, they're probably not going to see an audition notice in the paper. (Their parents will, though, and then word-of-mouth can do the rest!)
- Nearly everyone listens to the radio, but only in short stretches. Listenership is at its peak during "morning drive," when people are heading to work. As the day goes on, listenership decreases, then picks up during the afternoon drive home—but after that, it continues to dwindle. The audience gets younger as afternoon turns into evening.
- Nearly everyone watches TV, and they do it in big chunks, too. Viewership increases as the day goes on. There's a reason why 8:00 to 11:00 P.M. is called prime time: It's the prime time to catch the most viewers.
- The Web is a virtual made-for-young-people medium. Although they tend to use it mostly for fun, it's also their preferred medium for conducting research and keeping in touch. Adults use the Web, too, of course, and they're more apt to use it to look up information for purposes other than research projects.
- Different content appeals to different groups of people. The listenership of a Top 40 radio station varies from the listenership of a country or an R&B station. The same goes for cable TV. MTV viewers differ from Discovery Channel viewers or

Nickelodeon viewers. There's always some degree of audience overlap in TV and radio, but media programming is an art based on appealing to target audiences.

These factors all influence how and why you should buy ads, which we'll talk about more specifically as I focus on the individual forms of mass media in the next few chapters.

Things to Think About

- What does your company do to actively encourage word-of-mouth news about an event?
- What are the major mass media outlets in your area?
- Is there stiff competition among media outlets (for example, are there competing newspapers)?
- What uncontrolled media does your company typically use? Why?
- What controlled media does your company use?

For More Information

Statistics in the mass media section are from John Vivian's *The Media of Mass Communication* (5th ed. Boston: Allyn and Bacon, 1999), a highly readable text I use when teaching my Intro to Mass Media class. If you're interested in more information about the history and usage of the various media, I recommend it.

Newspaper Editors Don't Want to Be Your Friends (But They *Do* Want to Be Hooked)

friend recently bemoaned the tiny blurb his theatre company got about its latest production in the local paper. The notice was buried somewhere on the lifestyles page next to the scores from the ladies' bridge league. As it turned out, attendance for the show was lower than expected, and everyone looking for a reason turned the newspaper—and my friend, who had sent the notice to the newspaper—into the scapegoat.

"But it was Neil Simon," he told me.

Who, the assignment editor? I asked.

"No, the playwright," he said, either ignoring or overlooking my sarcasm.

Didn't he write *A Bunch of Plays People Love to See?*

"Of course," my friend said. "Everyone loves Neil Simon."

Everyone, that is, except the paper's assignment editor. True, Simon is a crowd-pleaser, but a newspaper editor isn't going to like Neil Simon just because he's Neil Simon. An editor *will* like Simon, though, if you give the editor a reason to like him.

The simple fact that your production is happening is news . . . but it's not big news. It deserves a short little write-up, but that's about all. If you're lucky, it won't get buried on the lifestyles page.

What were you expecting? I asked my friend.

"I was hoping for a picture," he said. "Maybe a nice feature story or something."

Have they given you that kind of coverage before?

"Last time, they did a big story for their Sunday leisure section. A picture and everything," he said. "The time before that, they did an interview with the playwright."

But that was the premiere of the playwright's first play, and the playwright was a hometown fellow. That's big news for a relatively small town. Newspapers love that kind of stuff. And the other play—the one that got the big story—tied into the theatre company's diversity celebration.

So, I asked, what was your hook for the Simon show?

"Hook?" he asked. I could tell by the look on his face he thought he was talking to Mr. Potato-Head. But his expression also made it oh-so-clear to me why publicity for the Simon play hadn't worked out as the theatre had hoped.

The Hook's the Thing

Newspaper editors want to be hooked. In journalism lingo, a *hook* is that unique facet of a story that hooks the audience. In your case, you want to hook the editor's interest. If you do that, I guarantee your story will hook readers' interest.

What makes a show unique? Well, that varies depending on the show, the production, the cast and crew, and the company. Perhaps you have an actor performing in her fiftieth production. Perhaps an award-winning set designer is coming out of a ten-year retirement for your show. Perhaps the play has a strong social theme and one of your goals for the production is to promote social awareness. Perhaps someone who's been making costumes for years and years and years has created especially notable costumes for the production.

Is Neil Simon a hook? By himself, no . . . unless he's coming to your town for the production: That's a hook. If Simon's nephew is the director, that's a hook. If this show is the first in a season-long retrospect of Simon's work, that's even a hook. (But by the time you publicize Simon show number two, you'll need to find a different hook.)

The hook doesn't need to be splashy and extravagant. It only needs to be different. It needs to turn a run-of-the-mill calendar listing into news.

"There needs to be some cool slant," says Beth Eberth, assistant editor of *The Times Herald* in Olean, New York. "Our newsroom has limited resources and people, and we have a lot of stories competing for space. We need to know why something is going to make an interesting story."

Inside the Newsroom

The Times Herald, with a daily circulation of around twenty thousand, is pretty typical of a small newspaper. The paper serves five rural counties along the border of western New York and Pennsylvania.

By midmorning, the newsroom is filled with the clatter of keyboards as reporters and editors rush to meet their 11:00 deadline. As the paper hits the press around lunchtime, the news staff finally has time to catch its collective breath and grab a bite to eat before buckling down to start the next day's stories.

"Our staff is half of what it was ten years ago," says Eberth. "We have less office space. We wrestle with those sorts of resource issues all the time." Unfortunately, most people don't realize that. After all, the typical newspaper prints more words each day than you find in an average novel. That's a lot of words. Some of those words might as well be about your show, right?

But look at it another way: Imagine having to publish a new novel every day, 365 days a year. Ugh.

Needless to say, reporters and editors have very little time. They always have two or three (or four or five) things going on, and they're always under deadline. The phones are ringing. The fax is beeping. Someone's Instant Messenger is making weird bloo-ding sounds in the background.

It's not surprising, then, that editors look for reasons to throw things away. Your press release is handwritten? Circular file. Full of typos? Circular file. The editor has to wade through a bunch of info and try to figure out what's important? Circular file.

That's why *it is crucial that you make things as easy as possible for editors.*

"The more work you make for us, the less info we'll put in," Eberth says. "We rely on the people supplying the information to pick out what's important. If you don't do it, we can't do it for you. You're the experts."

In *The Times Herald's* coverage area, nearly a dozen established arts-related groups compete for space in the paper, including four community theatres and two university theatre programs. Add in all the area high school choral, band, and drama programs . . . middle- and grade-school music programs . . . programs at area libraries . . . "They're all competing for space," says Eberth. "And those are just the arts-related things."

It's All in the Timing

Despite all the stories competing for coverage, the news business is still, in many ways, feast or famine. At times things hop like mad, while at others the newsroom coasts along. "If the paper is working on their Progress Edition, or it's high school graduation week, or if it's a couple of weeks before Christmas, those are really busy times," explains Eberth. "There are other times that are slow and we could use tips."

So, if you call the editor two days before high school graduation to pitch a story idea, chances are you'll get a curt "No," and your story will go to waste. But wait a week or two after graduation and you're likely to find the editor receptive to your idea.

Timing can also work in your favor when you can tie your theatre's activities into something else. It's always National Muskmelon Week or something like that. Find a way to tie into public awareness campaigns. Obviously, a natural would be National Community Theatre Month. But what about a play like *Wit* that could tie into Women's History Month? What if your show falls near Veterans Day? Could you have a preperformance ceremony to honor all the veterans who've participated in your shows over the years?

Those sorts of tie-ins make good hooks, and they can generate extra publicity. For instance, it's wise to arrange for a preshow photo that will appear in the newspaper a few days before opening. If it's National Chicken Wing Week, and you celebrate by holding a chicken barbecue before one of your matinees, that makes for another great photo opportunity.

The Bigger They Are . . .

Something else to consider is the size of the media market. Size does matter, but bigger is *not* better.

The bigger the media market, the less likely it is the major metro paper(s) will have an interest in your community theatre production. Small media outlets make their money on hometown stuff—people like to know who's up to what. It's the *Cheers* philosophy of news: Everyone who reads the local paper knows your name. Large media outlets don't have the luxury to take that approach because they have massive numbers of readers.

"Most editors won't touch community theatre," says Anthony Cardinale, a reporter and reviewer for *The Buffalo News* and the author of six professionally produced plays. *The Buffalo News* prints nearly a quarter of a million copies a day. Its daily circulation blankets the entire western portion of New York, stretching down beyond Olean and *The Times Herald* and into Pennsylvania.

"A lot of time, editors treat community theatres with disdain, even though some theatres do work of exceptional quality," Cardinale says. "Once in a great while, an editor might plug something with a picture, but they seldom do a feature. They're pretty busy covering the professional theatres in town."

Ida Scott, president of the Amherst Players, based in one of Buffalo's suburbs, knows exactly what Cardinale means. "It's easy to get lost in the shuffle here," Scott says. "It's not so much with the other community theatres in the Greater Buffalo area, but with the professional theatres downtown."

As a result of "the shuffle," the Amherst Players get virtually no coverage from *The Buffalo News*. "Unless we buy a paid ad," Scott says. "It's pretty expensive, and we don't think it warrants it."

The Buffalo News does offer a weekend calendar of events, however. "We publish our events in their Friday 'Gusto' section," Scott says. "We also list our shows in *Artvoice*, the biweekly arts paper, which has a calendar."

Scott's group does most of its publicity with *The Amherst Bee*, a weekly paper with a circulation of about 11,500 and an incredible loyalty among longtime residents, who generally tend to be settled, community-minded, and affluent. "The *Bee* will come out and do a picture for us," she says. The paper also has a weekly calendar, "BeeThere," that lists the Players' events.

For the Monmouth Community Players (MCP) in Monmouth, Maine, the story is similar. Their most thorough coverage comes from *The Capital Weekly*, a paper with a circulation of around 7,500. "They're more community oriented, so they're more apt to use our stuff," says MCP board member Lucy Rioux.

MCP is sandwiched midway between Lewiston, the state's second-largest media market, and Augusta, the state capital. The Lewiston *Sun-Journal* gives the group's productions some coverage, depending on how many cast members from Lewiston-Auburn are in the show, and Augusta's *Kennebec Journal* offers slightly better coverage because Monmouth is generally considered part of the Augusta metro area.

"*The Capital Weekly* is very fond of pictures," says Rioux. "In fact, they prefer to have a photo to go along with a story about one of our shows."

"We only have three reporters-slash-photographers, and we have to cover around twenty communities," explains Robert Long, editor of *The Capital Weekly*. "If a community theatre supplies us with a photo of decent quality, we'll run it along with info about their show."

Because the paper is a weekly, and it focuses on community events, a news story that appears one week may appear again—either whole or in edited form—the next week. Such is often the case with small weekly papers. "We let theatre companies know that if they get their promotional materials to us as early as possible, we'll try to give them multiple hits and run it two or three times," Long says.

Like most papers, *The Capital Weekly* runs a calendar of events, and Long makes it a point to list community theatre events. "I'll also run a photo or a press release about the theatre's show in a separate area in the paper to maximize the chance people will see the material," he says. "If they don't see it in one spot, they may see it in another."

Long goes out of his way, within reason, to help local theatre groups. Aside from MCP, there are five other groups he works with regularly, plus a number of school-related events. "We see it as part of our mission to help keep these groups alive," he explains. "We recognize that these groups have tight budgets, if any budgets at all, so we let them know we're available to help them promote their productions. It's an important part of what we do."

Making the News

In fact, most editors will happily help your theatre group—so long as you make it easy for them. "We know the people in our community," Eberth says. "We know they love their craft and we know how good they are at it. We like to give them what recognition we can."

Your job is to make it as easy as possible for editors to give your theatre that recognition. This has an important added bonus: By giving editors your message in a prewrapped form, you have more control over your own message. You have a greater chance to say exactly what *you* want to say about your production without relying on a reporter to say it for you.

Of course, you'd like to say everything you can about the show. But remember, you can't. There's just not enough space. So, your first step is to narrow your message:

- *What's important?* Obviously, the title and author, the company's name, when and where the show is being performed, and ticket information.
- *What's your hook?* What's your unique angle?
- *What facts develop that hook into a story?* The crucial distinction here is "facts that develop the hook into a story" versus facts that are related to the show but not necessarily related to the hook. Don't clutter the story with extraneous information: Keep it focused.
- *What's the show about?* The show synopsis should be no more than a paragraph and should be worked into the story smoothly.

Once you have your message narrowed down, there are a number of ways to get that message to the newspaper. The most important are press releases, photo opportunities, feature stories, and calendar listings. Personal interviews and press conferences are used less often. Some papers also print reviews.

Press Releases

Press releases are the primary way you'll get information to editors. A press release contains all the information an editor needs, organized from most to least important. Start with a short, concise lead paragraph. It should only be one or two sentences long and the information should be general: The Shepardstown Drama League

(SDL) will present Christopher Marlowe's *Doctor Faustus* at the Shepardstown Community Center next week.

Always include your company's full name in the lead, followed by the appropriate abbreviation. For example, a lead might say, "Next weekend, Albeeville Community Theatre (ACT) will present...." Then, on subsequent references to the theatre, you would simply use the acronym ACT.

The second paragraph in the release should include specific details about the show's time and place. Subsequent paragraphs should include a synopsis, quotes from the director or the theatre's president, and more details as necessary.

This is called the inverted pyramid style of newswriting. Big, broad information goes first, then, as the story progresses, the details get narrower and more specific. If editors need to cut something from a news story, they start at the end and work their way toward the beginning, chopping out the end of the story first because it's the less important material.

This is one reason why you should always finish a press release with a standard paragraph. The standard paragraph is two or three sentences that say something about your theatre company. It could be a quick history, an adaptation of your mission statement, or something similar. If your release gets edited, the first thing to go is your standard paragraph, which is the least important information (at least in relation to information in the release).

Occasionally, your release may get printed in its entirety. This sometimes happens when an editor has space to fill and nothing pressing to fill it. In that case, your standard paragraph gets printed, reminding the public who your theatre is and what it's about. In other words, the standard paragraph is a great way to slip in a plug.

Quotes are another way to slip in a plug for the theatre, but a good editor can recognize a self-congratulatory quote a mile away. Quotes that explain something or add new information are useful; quotes like "This is going to be a great show!" are terrible. *Of course* your director is going to say it's a great show. Use quotes to tell readers something they don't know or expect.

Unless Lawrence Olivier is coming back from the dead to do a performance with your company, a press release should not exceed two pages. That includes all the space you have to leave at the top of the first page. Don't waste an editor's time. Keep it brief. Only the most extraordinary circumstances warrant a longer release.

Another crucial item is proofreading. Triple-check things like times and dates and the spellings of names.

A press release should be sent to a newspaper at least ten working days before you want it to run. Build in some lead time, too. If you're sending a release about a show opening, you want the release to appear a few days before the opening. For instance, if opening night is Friday, you want the release to appear in the paper Tuesday or Wednesday. If you start counting back from there, that means you must send the release out two full weeks before opening. Few things annoy editors more than when you call them at the last minute and say, "Can I get this press release in tomorrow's paper?" A gracious editor may do it for you once or twice, but I'm warning you now: Don't push your luck.

Finally, you might want to check with the editor to see if the paper accepts press releases submitted via email. At the dawn of the e-age, this was a big no-no, but more often than not, editors will now accept something sent by email—if for no other reason than it saves someone the hassle of retyping text or scanning it in. Be sure to find out the editor's preferred format. Should the release be pasted into the body of an email or attached as a word processing document? What word processing program does the paper use? Is it on a Mac or PC platform? Finding out such details takes time, but it can save time in the long run.

Sample press releases are included in the appendix, including sample standard paragraphs. Pay attention to the format, which is designed to make life easier for the editor. The content of a press release is primarily aimed at the general public; the format is primarily aimed at the editor.

Photo Opportunities

Theatre is a visual art, so it lends itself well to pictures. When you call a newspaper and ask it to include a photo, specify a couple of good photo ideas. Just make sure you call well in advance so the editor has several days to make a photo assignment.

Again, build in some lead time. Don't wait until the night before opening. Your show may make an interesting feature, but if hard news breaks, the photographer may have to cancel your photo in order to go cover the explosion or the effigy-burning downtown. If that happens, you're out of luck. Give yourself an extra day or two so you have time to reschedule if necessary.

Have an extra copy of the news release ready to give to the photographer. You may have already sent one to the paper, but have an extra ready for the photographer because it could make life easier for the editor. After all, you don't want the editor to have to hunt for the original if it's been misplaced.

When you're choosing your shot, an easy trap to fall into is "We need to take pictures of the leads." While that's great for egos, it might not make for great pictures. Take a picture of something interesting. Two people sitting on a couch chatting does not make an interesting picture. A person delivering a monologue does not look interesting (unless it's Hamlet talking to a skull). However, two people sword fighting looks interesting. Someone hooked up to a heap of medical equipment looks interesting. A man-eating plant puppet looks interesting.

Don't pose your actors, either. If you do, they'll look . . . well, posed. Let them run through part of a scene. Give them something to do and say. Let the photographer capture them in action. The picture will look much more alive and interesting.

If the paper can't send a photographer, offer to submit a photo with a press release. Have someone take several photos so the paper has several shots to choose from. Use black-and-white film if at all possible because it reproduces much better on newsprint than color film does. Make sure you put a caption on the back of each photo. Identify the people, from left to right, and explain what they're doing. Include the show's title and performance dates and times.

You may on occasion have the opportunity to do a photo that does not directly relate to a show. Maybe you get a big donation. Maybe your company brings a well-known actor to town to give a talk. These types of events let you keep your theatre in the public eye between shows, which is always a good thing. Just *make sure the pictures are interesting.* Check presentations are boring (even if you use those goofy giant checks); in fact, many papers don't print check presentations or ribbon cuttings because they're dull. People talking at podiums are equally dull. Think of something interesting.

Chapter 14 offers some picture-taking tips. Examples of good and bad photographs are printed in the Appendix.

Feature Stories

Here's where a good hook pays off. A feature story takes a good hook and develops it into a longer piece. Feature stories are also called human-interest stories. They tend to get accompanied by photos, and they often get preferential, prominent layout on a page. They get a lot of attention.

If you want to pitch a feature story idea to your local paper, give the paper a month's lead time. When you call, make sure your hook is good and be ready to answer a lot of questions. If the editor goes for it, be prepared to schedule a time when a reporter can come talk to you, the director, or the subject of the feature.

If you're extremely lucky, and if you have a writer who's good enough, the local paper might let you submit your own feature story about the show. You can sometimes submit photos with a story, as well. This means more work for you, but it's actually the ideal situation: You get to tell the story the way you want to, and you get lots of good ink. And because you do all the work, it makes the editor's life easier.

An editor usually accepts feature submissions only after a PR person has established a good working relationship with the editor—and, of course, if the PR person has publication-quality writing skills. Otherwise, feature submissions will seem like clutter to an editor.

An example of a feature can be found in the Appendix.

Calendar Listings

Calendar listings are similar to press releases, but they boil everything down to who, what, where, why, when, and how much. The important thing to keep in mind with calendar listings is that some newspapers require them as much as a month and a half in advance. Give yourself plenty of lead time for your calendar listings. If you send a listing early, that's one less thing for you to worry about as you get closer to show time.

See the Appendix for an example.

Personal Interviews

A personal interview is an opportunity to sit one-on-one with a reporter and offer information. Community theatres tend to build their publicity around shows, so opportunities for personal interviews generally relate to feature stories.

But a smart PR plan that gives your theatre a steadier presence in the media can use personal interviews to great advantage. For instance, if your new season has a strong social theme, you might invite a reporter to spend a half hour chatting with your president or artistic director, who can talk about the importance of the social theme, why your company decided to adopt it, etc.

Because of the time demands newspapers are under, you may get one personal interview a year if you're lucky.

Press Conferences

Typically, press conferences are saved only for major news. After all, you're asking a bunch of reporters to take time out of their busy day to listen to what you have to say. It had better be good.

Press conferences call a lot of attention to something. If you do them willy-nilly, they'll quickly lose their impact, and editors will start to turn a deaf ear to what you have to say. Then, when something really big does happen, you'll be the Theatre Company that Cried Wolf, and you may get ignored altogether.

It's important to keep in mind what "major news" means. For most community theatres, a gift of ten thousand dollars would be major news. But in a newspaper's eyes, that's not major news. If you've conducted an economic impact study with other area arts groups and found you pump a combined two million dollars annually into the local economy, that might merit a press conference, especially if you need an economist to explain the finer details of the study.

When you schedule a press conference, remember to keep in mind your local paper's deadline. If it's a daily paper that comes out in the afternoon, the deadline is usually around 11:00 A.M. You don't want to have your press conference midmorning or you'll drive the editor nuts. Shoot for first thing in the morning for that day's edition, or late afternoon for the next day's edition.

If your daily paper is a morning paper, a late-afternoon press conference works fine, but a morning press conference can be tough: Most reporters don't come in to work until after lunch because they work until 11:00 P.M. or even beyond midnight.

For weekly papers, keep in mind what day the paper comes out. If the paper comes out every Tuesday, exciting news offered at a press conference on Wednesday turns into old news by the next issue. On the other hand, a press conference late Monday afternoon would probably miss the deadline.

Reviews

When a paper prints a review, it does so as a courtesy to the community theatres it serves. Yes, reviews serve a function for the general public: People read a review to help them decide whether or not to go see a show. But reviews put newspapers in a difficult position.

Should the reviewer be honest and say what she really thinks about the show? In other words, should she talk about the good, the bad, and the ugly parts of the show? If she does, the Theatre People get upset. The reviewer and the editor have to see those Theatre People in the supermarket and at the bank. That can get awkward if a review says something that's less than complimentary.

"They don't want a review, they want ink," says *The Buffalo News's* Tony Cardinale. "But who does that really serve?"

If a reviewer says only nice things, intentionally slanting the review to stress the positive, is the review really helping readers make up their minds? And if it's not truly serving the public's interest, is it worth printing? Theatre companies, of course, say yes. After all, a theatre company can get a lot of miles from a good review in the paper.

Some papers refuse to run reviews because they don't want to be placed in a position where they might have to compromise honesty for the sake of keeping the peace. They don't want the headache of angry townspeople storming the gates of the newsroom with torches and pitchforks.

If you're lucky enough to be in a town where the paper will run a review, be nice to them about it. The paper is doing your theatre a favor. If the reviewer says something that isn't quite stellar, chances are that your director thinks the show is better than it really is, anyway. Chalk it up to experience and be happy about the twelve other reviews the paper has published that have all been glowing.

That might be a tough pill to swallow, but the newspaper business can be full of bad medicine.

The Hard Lessons

Some other potentially tough-to-swallow bits of information to keep in mind when dealing with newspapers:

- *No one is as interested in theatre as Theatre People are.* We love theatre. That's why we do it. We put in long hours and don't get paid for it, so—rightly so—we figure we deserve a little credit. But other things appeal more to newspaper readers than theatre does. That means you have to think in broad terms: What is it about your show that would interest people who might not otherwise be interested in theatre?

■ *In a newspaper, space is money.* Editorial boards devote space to ads, which make money from advertisers, and news, which makes money from readers who buy the paper to read the news. Unless you're willing to fork over money for an ad, you need to convince editors your show is news. Otherwise, they're not going to just give away their most valuable asset, no matter how much you think they ought to. "We don't have the space to give everyone what they want," says *The Times Herald*'s Beth Eberth.

■ *Your news coverage is not tied to the amount of advertising you buy.* There's a myth that a paper will give you better coverage if you buy ad space. This simply isn't true (at least in most places). At all but the smallest newspapers, the advertising and news departments are run separately from each other. While an advertising person might tell you "Let me talk to the news editor about a story" when you're buying an ad, most editors would be *highly* offended if you suggested their coverage could be bought.

Making Contact

When it's finally time for you to make that call to the newsroom, keep in mind the following:

■ Make things as easy as possible for the editor.
■ Be professional but friendly.
■ Ask if the editor is under deadline. If so, find out when a convenient time would be for you to call back.
■ Be concise. Use that hook.
■ Before you send that press release, proofread, proofread, proofread. Spellcheck, spellcheck, spellcheck.

"Don't be shy," adds *The Capital Weekly*'s Robert Long. "It seems a strange thing to say to theatre people, but some people seem hesitant.

Go to the news people at your local paper and let them know you need help getting the word out."

Other Press

While most community theatres focus their energy on the local newspaper, other print venues can get overlooked.

- *College newspapers.* Are there any college newspapers in your area? If so, students from the college probably participate in your productions. (If not, why not?) Send press releases to the college paper, whether any students are involved or not.
- *Hometowners.* A hometowner is a press release you send to the hometown newspaper of someone who's participating in the production. This pertains mostly to college students who appear in or work backstage for a show. Why not send a short press release to the student's hometown paper mentioning the student's involvement? Papers almost always use hometowners (back again to the *Cheers* philosophy of news). Distributing hometowners may not help drum up much audience for you, especially if the student's hometown is far away, but it does generate goodwill with the student, who is apt to come back and perform with you again if you make him feel wanted and appreciated. If he comes back, his friends will also come back to see him perform, which translates into ticket sales. An example of a hometowner appears in the Appendix.
- *Weekly advertising circulars.* Many communities have something like the *Pennysaver* or the *Weekly Shopper*. These publications sell ads to businesses, which often advertise exclusive offers to readers. The circulars are distributed free. Circulars sometimes include calendars of events, and they also sometimes give breaks on their rates to nonprofit groups.

It's All in the Placement (The Secret to Newspaper Advertising)

Take a look at your local newspaper. Where are the ads? At the bottom of the page, right? Do the ads jump out at you? Honestly?

If it's a page with a bunch of smaller ads, the ads are probably stacked up in a corner, with the largest ad serving as a building block around which others are placed.

Even worse are pages with a plethora of small ads, one column wide by one inch tall, that advertise local barbecues, which bands are playing at which bars, and where the week's bingo games are being played. The ads all have different borders. Some have rounded corners. Some have black fill with white letters. It all looks quite busy; the ads fight each other for your attention.

The disadvantage to newspaper ads is that people tend to skip over them. We know where the ads are going to be on any given newspaper page, so many people unconsciously block out those parts of the page and only look at the stuff that's interesting.

So how can your ad stand out and grab attention? Take a look again at the ads in your paper. Which ones catch your eye? Probably the ones that have a lot of visual contrast, right?

Contrast works in several ways:

- A lot of white space in an ad separates your text from the busy newspaper around it. The empty space might seem like a waste, but it actually serves as a highly effective attention grabber. People tend to want to cram a lot of information into an ad because it costs so much money, but often you'll be better served by going with less text and more white space. Less is more.
- Big, bold letters contrast with the typically small text of a newspaper, but they also need to contrast with the typeface used for the paper's headlines.
- Graphics and pictures contrast with words.

Where your ad appears in the paper also makes a huge difference. The sports section is usually a bad spot. Wrong audience. I once had an ad rep suggest, enthusiastically, "Maybe I should put it on the page where we have all our band listings for the weekend." Again, wrong audience. As soon as I pointed that out, she said, "Oh, yeah, I guess you're right."

Believe it or not, ads placed near the obituaries are generally effective. In a small newspaper, everyone reads the obituaries.

Spend some time talking with your ad rep at the paper. Explain your needs and who your audience is. Usually, your ad rep can help find the best placement for your ad, and that makes all the difference.

Ads are measured in, and ad rates are based on, column-inches. Translated, that's one column wide by one inch tall. So, for instance, an ad that spans two columns and measures five inches tall totals ten column-inches. That's actually a pretty good ad size. Anything much bigger turns into an expensive investment.

Instead of size, spend your newspaper advertising money on repetition. A bigger ad run once only gets seen one day, if it's seen at all. If you repeat the ad, you increase the chances that a particular reader will see it. For people who see the ad multiple times, you reinforce the message.

Things to Think About

- What can you do to make life easier for an editor?
- What's your hook?
- Are you providing the paper with enough lead time to do what you're asking?
- Have you had an extra set of eyes (or two sets) proofread your press releases?
- Can you tie in to particular events or public awareness campaigns for extra publicity?
- Does your area have alternative newspapers?
- Who is your audience? How does that affect the placement of your ads?

For Further Information

If you're going to be writing press releases, make things easier for the editor by learning to speak and write "newsroom." Get a copy of *The Associated Press Stylebook and Libel Manual,* a reference guide that spells out newsroom rules for punctuation, spelling, and the use of courtesy titles (Mr., Ms., etc.) and abbreviations, and includes a slew of other tricks of the newswriting trade.

Quest for the Holy Grail (The Magazine Feature)

When a newspaper has long ago gone the way of the birdcage liner, a magazine still holds its spot on the coffee table, or on the end table next to the recliner, or on top of the back of the toilet.

A magazine's staying power stems from the way it's written. People have to settle in and devote a chunk of time to reading a magazine, so the writing must make that time commitment worthwhile. It does so by providing in-depth reporting, interesting features, and colorful pictures. Most magazines also have a special focus targeted at a specific audience.

The magazines community theatres deal with are usually regional magazines based out of a metro area. They appeal to people who have an interest in the lifestyles of that particular geographic region (as magazines go, that's a relatively broad focus). Readership for regional magazines is typically middle- and upper-class professionals with some disposable income.

Sounds like our kind of people, doesn't it?

Well, don't start drooling yet. I've gotta tell you, good coverage in a magazine is the Holy Grail of community theatre PR.

I'm not talking about a listing in the calendar of events. Most metro and regional magazines have some sort of calendar, and it's pretty easy to get your event listed there. Just follow the submission guidelines printed with the calendar. When writing up your entry, copy the format used in the calendar itself (or follow the example in the Appendix).

No, when I talk about the Grail, I'm talking about the magazine feature story.

Getting Coverage

Because regional magazines appeal to relatively broad audiences, editors get quite selective about their content. Your story idea needs to be so unique and interesting and sexy that it's going to be of interest to non-theatregoers. It has to wow the editor and be something that will wow the readers.

Coverage may also depend on a magazine's theme. You might have a great idea, but if it doesn't jibe with the other material in a particular issue, it won't make the cut.

Another factor that influences magazine coverage is the magazine's raison d'être.

Most magazines exist for profit reasons. Some exist for propaganda purposes. Some exist as an extension of an educational mission.

San Marco Magazine, based in Jacksonville, Florida, exists for a promotional purpose. "We were created by the San Marco Merchants' Association as a way to promote this area of the city," explains publisher Jennifer Price.

The glossy, digest-sized magazine, published quarterly, has a print run of around twenty thousand. Copies are distributed free across northern Florida. "It promotes San Marco as a destination, so that people feel like they can't come to Jacksonville without coming to this part of the city," Price says. "The goal is to increase traffic to San Marco, to increase business, and to increase property values."

Price characterizes her audience as high-end readers who are interested in history and culture ... and who like to shop. Those are educational and economic demographics that match up with theatregoers.

Recognizing the overlap in audience demographics, *San Marco Magazine* and Theatre Jacksonville have worked out a trade agreement. "We give them tickets, which they can then give away to their other clients," explains Theatre Jacksonville's marketing director, Tony Allegretti. "We also give them an ad in our playbill. In exchange, they give us advertising in the magazine and they list our events in their calendar."

Price says she's open to further collaboration. "I do like to support the people and businesses who support the magazine," she says.

While *San Marco Magazine* hasn't done a big feature story on Theatre Jacksonville, the theatre has cropped up in cameo roles in other features. "We're doing a story on ghosts in the fall," Price says. "Theatre Jacksonville has a stage ghost, of course, so they'll be in that issue."

No big feature story, though? Allegretti expects it'll happen someday; for now, Price says she's overloaded for content. Hmmm. The quest continues . . .

One Shot

Something else to keep in mind about magazine coverage: You only get one shot at it. Once a magazine has covered you, you're done for a while. You'll still get calendar listings, but don't expect article after article, no matter how great your ideas are.

If the Goldoni Civic Players (GCP) restore a dilapidated theatre to its original splendor as a centerpiece for downtown Goldoni, that's a "wow" idea. Say the regional magazine does a beautiful cover story on the theatre and on GCP. If GCP brings Arthur Miller to town next season, the magazine *may* do a story on the playwright, but GCP won't be a centerpiece of the story for sure. The story has been done.

That's because GCP *is* the first story: How it came up with the idea to restore the theatre, how it raised the money, how it carried out the work, what it plans to do with the theatre. GCP, GCP, GCP—get it? The renovation is only the angle. Once you say all that stuff about GCP, what new things could you possibly say about GCP for the Arthur Miller story? *He* would be the next story, not GCP, because there are plenty of things about Mr. Miller that the magazine's readers haven't ever read.

It's important for you to give magazine coverage careful consideration in your PR planning. Come up with your "wow" idea and use it as a hook to open doors to other publicity. Make the most of your opportunity. The theatre is the story. Once a magazine has done the story, years will pass before they revisit it.

Mind you, it is possible to get multiple mentions over a year or two in a magazine's news and notes section. Such sections usually consist of a couple of pages of short little newsy blurbs. It's a place to send your really great ideas that don't quite measure up to the "wow" level. Such news and notes entries consist of only two or three paragraphs, so don't overwhelm editors with details. Study the writing style of the blurbs the magazine publishes, then try to emulate them when you're writing your submission.

Alternative Alternatives

While a lot of metro areas have slick, glossy magazines, most smaller areas don't. Something most places do have, though, are 'zines. 'Zines aren't quite magazines (which explains why the name's abbreviated like it is). 'Zines are periodicals produced on lower budgets, usually on a lower grade of paper and with less color, and they usually have an "underground" feel to them. 'Zines often present alternative or nonmainstream points of view, and their readership tends to be extremely loyal.

'Zines traditionally target hip younger folks. It's a much different audience than the upper-income folks who'll pick up a slick, glossy magazine. Without even reading the articles, you can tell the difference by looking at the ads: A 'zine has ads for rock concerts, clubs, salons, entertainment, piercing and tattooing, and personal injury lawyers, as well as singles ads.

While you can buy ads, most 'zines also have calendars of events and most do reviews. But let me warn you, if you invite someone from a 'zine to review your show, don't expect a warm and fuzzy commentary. If your theatre features avant-garde, edgy, or political material, a 'zine is a great place to promote your shows. If you're doing *Mame,* you might want to look at more traditional publications.

Not all 'zines go for the in-your-face attitude, though, particularly in rural areas, where people are generally less in-your-face. One such publication, *The Muse,* is one of the most popular publications in the counties south of Buffalo, New York, with readership stretching down into northwestern Pennsylvania. *The Muse,* according to its cover price, is priceless. Copies are distributed freely to readers because ad sales underwrite production costs.

Measuring eight by ten inches, *The Muse* is printed on newsprint with two-color artwork on the cover and one-color printing on the inside.

"*The Muse's* audience is varied, but if I had to characterize it, I'd say it's mostly comprised of females aged twenty-four to sixty-five," says senior editor Leslie Vincen. "Since women are usually the decision makers when it comes to choosing an outing, it makes sense that they would be interested in picking up *The Muse* to check out performances, restaurants, arts presentations, and shopping."

Vincen chooses content for *The Muse* in accordance with the publication's mission to provide cultural information about the community to the community's readers. When deciding on articles, she gives priority to cultural organizations such as theaters, dance groups, writers groups, libraries, arts associations, visual arts groups, and musical presenters. "*The Muse* will sometimes offer an article space to an organization or provide a space when asked," Vincen adds. "All are based on timeliness and availability."

That offer of space essentially turns *The Muse* into a form of controlled media. A theatre does its own write-up about a show and Vincen, with a little tweaking for style, prints the article as is.

"We can feature an advertisement, an article, and a calendar listing about the community theatre performance all in the same month," Vincen says. "That issue may sit on someone's coffee table for weeks until the next one comes out, and it may be read many times over by many people. A magazine that someone picks up for the express purpose of getting cultural information already has a built-in advantage."

The Last Word

Don't spend a whole lot of time trying to get feature stories about your theatre in the local magazine. It's wisest to set it as a long-term goal and then wait for the right opportunity.

When you do get coverage, it'll offer your theatre high-profile publicity. It'll also be a huge morale booster for your board and volunteers. Therefore, use magazine coverage to really strut your stuff as an *organization,* not just as a producer of plays or of a particular play.

Magazine coverage is, after all, the Grail. If you can find it, drink deeply and get as much from it as you can.

Things to Think About

- What magazines and 'zines exist in your area?
- What is the geographic range of each publication?
- How does your artistic programming mesh with the attitudes of those publications?
- What has your theatre done in the past two to three years that would qualify as a "wow" idea?
- What's coming up that might be a "wow" idea?

6   Radio Daze

I can't begin to tell you how many times I've written a script for a radio ad and the client has said, "Put the phone number in there. Gotta have the phone number."

You don't want the phone number in there, I'd respond.

"Sure! How else're they gonna get in touch with us?" the client would invariably ask in a self-assured manner.

How are they going to write your phone number down, I'd counter, trying my hardest not to sound patronizing...but probably failing.

"With a pen."

With a pen. Hmmm. Think about that for a second. As a general rule, do people listen to the radio with pens in their hands?

They're busy driving. Or eating. Or typing. Or scrubbing their underarms with a washcloth in the shower. The fact is, people listen to the radio *while they do other things,* which makes radio a secondary medium. Long gone are the evenings when families sat around the living room and listened to the radio. Nowadays, the radio may be on, but it doesn't command our undivided attention.

But usually I didn't have to explain that to the client. My raised eyebrows and skeptical look said enough. By that point, the client had realized he doesn't listen to the radio with a pen in hand, either. But he still hoped for the best—maybe his commercial would be so brilliant it would have people leaping out of their chairs and across the room to get a pen.

Now, my ads were pretty good—but not *that* good. But even if they were, by the time a listener got a pen and something to write on, the commercial would be over, or at least nearly so. And radio isn't like the newspaper, where you can go back and look for the number: Once it's said, it's gone. So there you are, with a pen and a scrap of paper, listening to the next commercial. Maybe you can get *that* phone number instead.

I would be lying if I said people don't put phone numbers in radio commercials (called "spots"). You hear phone numbers on the radio all the time. But that doesn't make it a good idea. After all, how many numbers do *you* write down?

Instead of stressing a phone number, I recommend reinforcing your *name* in listeners' minds. If they can remember your name, most intelligent people will realize: "I can look up their phone number in the phone book."

I'm not just ranting about a pet peeve. This whole phone number business illustrates two crucial things you need to keep in mind about radio: It's secondary and it's transitory.

So why do theatres use radio? As we discussed in Chapter 3, there are many good reasons, the most important of which is that radio is everywhere. In a very literal sense, we're bombarded with radio waves all the time. But unless we have the right dental work in our back teeth, we can't pick up those signals without the help of clock radios, car stereos, boom boxes, streaming audio on websites, the entertainment centers in our living rooms, and, of course, good old transistor radios.

On a practical level, theatre PR people can use radio because it's so versatile. For example, we can use it for

- advertising
- underwriting
- talk show interviews

- in-studio guests
- news stories
- public service announcements (PSAs)
- sponsorships
- ticket giveaways

I'll talk about each one in a bit more depth, but first, let's try and figure out which stations to use.

The Secret to Radio Advertising

Because radio is secondary and transitory, the secret to success, particularly with advertising, is *repetition*. If you send out your message enough times, people are bound to hear it. Repetition also reinforces your message.

Buying enough radio spots to blanket your community can be tough, though, because it can get costly. That's why it's important to know which stations reach which listeners. Don't choose a station just because you or the folks on your board like it, choose it because your audience likes it. It may well be that your audience members listen to the same station you do—like-minded people tend to like similar things—but you want to base the choice on research, not personal preference.

Stations themselves can give you some of the information you need, but you should also do a little research on your own before you approach any of them. Here's how to start:

- Make a list of the radio stations in your area. Which are based in your hometown? Which are based in nearby towns? Which are based a good distance away? Include both FM and AM stations.
- Pay close attention to the format of each station. What type of music does each station play? How much news does each station offer? When and how often is the news offered? Are there any public service programs? Interview programs? Do the DJs ever have guests on the air with them?
- Pay attention to which stations run contests. How often do they give away prizes? What kinds of prizes are they?

- Get an idea of how powerful each station is. How far does its signal go? Is it immediate, just in town, or does it broadcast over vast distances?

If you examine information about the radio stations along with the information you have about your audience, you can start whittling down your choices.

For instance, if your audience primarily comes from a twenty-mile radius, then what's the sense of advertising on a station whose signal hits a seventy-five-mile radius? Yes, you might attract someone from that larger area, but it's more cost-effective to try and reach them through a newspaper. Just because a radio station has a huge reach doesn't mean it's the best station for you.

As the saying goes, "It's not the size of your broadcast tower, it's what you do with it." In other words, broadcast range doesn't matter nearly as much as format. Format is the number one reason people listen to a particular station. Who cares if the station's signal reaches ten thousand people. if the listeners are all stock-car racing fans? I'm certain there are racing fans who enjoy live theatre a great deal, but for the most part, it's a safe bet to assume you're looking at two separate audiences there.

If your audience is older and more conservative, the nearest public radio affiliate will probably be more appropriate than the local classic rock station. For a slightly younger crowd of professionals, adult contemporary is effective. It's also the format you hear most often in businesses. Country music, on the other hand, is not especially effective. Think of the stereotypes—pardon the pun—and you get an idea of which music formats appeal to which people.

Something else to consider: Stations that rebroadcast satellite-based programming aren't as effective as stations that generate their programming locally. A key ingredient to radio success is to think local, local, local.

Advertising Versus Underwriting

Similar to advertising, but specific to public radio stations, is underwriting. Simply put, you give a public radio station a gift and, in return, they mention you as a supporter of the station.

· It doesn't sound like much, but in recent years the mentions stations offer have become much more elaborate and, dare I say it, commercial (gasp!). A station doesn't just mention your theatre's name, it also reads a short blurb about your company. That's where you slip in information about your next show.

According to Linda Clark, an account executive with public radio station WITF-FM in Harrisburg, Pennsylvania, the Federal Communications Commission (FCC) has specific guidelines about underwriting credits. "We can identify the corporate donor, but the credits cannot be promotional in nature," she explains. "The question be-' comes 'What is promotional and what isn't?'"

Some rules of thumb for underwriting:

- Credits that include a call to action are a no-no. For instance, you can't say "Buy your tickets now!" or "Reserve your seats today."
- Credits can't include anything comparative—for example, "The *oldest* theatre in the area."
- Avoid credits that include subjective language, like "the funniest show" or "the best company in town."
- Don't say anything that can't be proven. For example, you can't really guarantee a show offers "guaranteed nonstop laughter."

Your account executive at the radio station will help you craft a credit. A typical example might sound something like this:

> The Little Theatre of Beckettsburg, presenting the Shakespearean comedy 'As You Like It,' May 24th through the 27th, with nightly performances at 7:30 P.M., in the Edson Center for the Arts.

It sounds like little more than a public service announcement, right? So why bother? Because public radio listeners are more affluent and have higher education levels than the average listener of a commercial station, and they participate in a broader array of interests. Any station's sales reps will be able to give you information about why that station might work for you. WITF is a National Public Radio affiliate that features classical music. According to the station's sales sheet, its listeners are 92 percent more likely to attend live theatre than the average person.

"Over half of a public radio station's audience is typically made up of people who hold positions in middle and upper management,"

Clark says. That's important because you're not only reaching potential audience members, you're reaching community leaders . . . and
potential donors. "They are charitable givers, and they give at higher
levels and with more frequency than the average person," Clark
adds. "That's another good reason to get your message in front of
them."

Sam Kuba of Theatre Harrisburg in Pennsylvania can't say
enough good things about the results his theatre gets from underwriting: "Other [advertising] things are sort of peripheral. We've stuck
with what got us where we are . . . and that's public radio."

Theatre Harrisburg and WITF have also worked out a ticket
exchange deal. "We have to make a certain level of purchase in cash,
but they like to do things for their other clients," Kuba explains, "so
I give them 250 tickets to a show or something, and then they give
the equivalent value of airtime. I get about half of my radio airtime
comped to me."

Clark says it's a lucrative deal for everyone involved. "Theatre
Harrisburg isn't the only group that does it, either," she says. "We
probably make one hundred thousand dollars a year in gifts from
arts and cultural groups."

Underwriting, like advertising, costs money. You can also take
advantage of radio in other—free!—ways. An extremely effective way
is through on-air interviews.

Interviewing the Interviewers

Some stations have interview shows. Others have special guests in the
studio during drive time. Others do phone interviews. Whatever the
time or occasion, a radio interview is a great way to send a controlled,
or at least semicontrolled, message to listeners.

"Because it's theatre, because it's entertainment, we absolutely
should support anything in the arts. It's one of us," says Marie
Costello, morning cohost at WESB in Bradford, Pennsylvania, a
rural town of about ten thousand people. Costello also hosts the
daily *LiveLine* talk show during the lunch hour.

"The arts, and community theatre in particular, enhance our
community because they show diversity," she says. "Smaller towns
tend to be more homogenous, so theatre is a good way to get some
insight into the world outside the four walls of the community. It's

also extremely important to our youth to show them they can do something bigger than Bradford."

First Impressions

Because Bradford is a small town, with a small-town way of doing things, Costello says, interpersonal relationships are extremely important. "When someone calls me up and wants to be on the *LiveLine,* it really turns me off if they talk down to me," she says. "Sometimes they act like 'Oh, this is theatre,' and 'la-dee-da-da.' If they tick me off, I'm not going to put them on the show. I tell them my schedule is booked. And there isn't anywhere else they can do an interview and get the kind of impact they would get here, because we're the only game in town."

Likewise, if the contact person is nice, Costello is much more apt to put her on the air, "even if it's not something big and splashy," she says. "I always ask myself, 'Is this worthwhile? Is this something I want to promote?' Can I believe in it and truthfully say, 'This sounds great'? If it's something I can believe in, then it's probably something my audience can believe in."

Patricia Madden, host of the weekly *Arts Connection* on public radio station WMFE-FM in Orlando, Florida, also wonders what's in it for her audience when someone asks to be on her program.

"There are *so* many groups, and *so* many people want to be on," she says. Because she's in a much larger market than Costello is, Madden has a much more formal approach to booking her guests. "I want to be fair and objective," she explains. "When you work with a guest who's unprofessional, it makes it tough."

Madden agrees with Costello that first impressions are crucial: "When you approach the media for an inquiry, make sure you create an interest. Explain 'Here's why you should have us on.' Definitely don't call and say 'You *must* do this.' You don't want to alienate or put a person off."

Preshow Prep

Madden's program covers a wide array of arts, from amateur and professional theatre to visual arts to music and poetry. "Orlando is not known for its arts community; it's known as a tourist town," she says. "But central Florida has a vibrant arts scene."

Madden approaches her show with what she calls "a childlike sense of wonder." Therefore, although she does extensive research on each guest, she doesn't give guests suggestions about what to discuss or what to prepare. "I get them, in the course of the interview, to show me what they're doing," she says. "It's about the artists—and I'm also an artist, so this is not really straight journalism. It's a conversation."

Costello, on the other hand, likes to go into an interview with more information. "Educate your host ahead of time, without being patronizing. Don't just assume she's as familiar with your production as you are," she says. "Offer some focus for the interviewer: 'We're doing a fund drive, and we're going to announce the season, so that's what we want to talk about.'"

But at the same time, be prepared to talk about anything: the show, the company, yourself. "I think it's pretty interesting when my guest is an accountant by day and he does this acting stuff at night. I like to find out what makes a guy like that tick," Costello says.

Certainly, Costello and Madden take different approaches as they prepare for an interview. The folks at your local station will have their own way of doing things, too. When you make your initial contact, being as friendly and professional as possible, *ask if the host wants anything from you prior to the interview*. That way, everyone's bases are covered.

Scheduling

When it comes to booking an appearance, Madden and Costello offer the same cautionary advice: Be aware of scheduling demands. Shows book up quickly, so time is at a premium. "Make sure you approach hosts in a way that takes those demands into account," Madden says.

"You can't call two days ahead of time and say 'Can you get me on?'," Costello adds. "Call *well* in advance."

Who to Send

When arranging a radio interview, one of the most important things to consider is who to send from your theatre. Often, the first impulse is to send the president of the organization, the director of the upcoming show, or one of the lead actors.

One of the important functions of a theatre's president is to serve as a figurehead and cheerleader, so the occasional radio appearance is a good opportunity for some exposure. The president should be able to speak about any and all aspects of the company, including current and past activities, the personnel, and special projects.

Radio interviews often come just before a particular production, so it's natural to recruit an actor or two to do some public appearances. People assume all actors like to talk, but that's not always the case. Don't pick someone just because she is the lead; instead, choose someone who'll be engaging and fun. Nothing is worse for an interviewer than interviewing someone who can't carry on an interesting conversation. "And prima donnas are a *definite* no-no," says Costello.

Try thinking of other folks who might make good interviews. If costumes play a big role in the show and the costumer likes to chat, arrange for him to do part of the interview. Look for other interesting people besides just the actors.

The key thing is to choose people who will come across as enthusiastic and glad to be there. If it sounds like they're having fun in the studio, listeners are much more apt to be engaged by the interview. And if they get engaged, they're more apt to buy a ticket.

One last tip: Be sure to talk into the microphone. Don't be afraid to lean into it, even; the person running the control panel—the operating board—can always turn you down if you're too loud. Too often, guests in the studio sit too far from the microphones, especially if several people are huddled around one mic, and it gets hard to hear them.

News and PSAs

Another way to get free radio exposure is through newscasts. News is the number two reason people listen to the radio (music is number one).

In bigger metropolitan areas, getting news coverage for your production can be tough, if not impossible. Metro areas have a lot of hard news, stuff like fires, accidents, crime, disasters, and politics. On top of that, most music stations don't devote a whole lot of time to news. The result is that a lot of news gets crammed into a few two-minute chunks.

Smaller areas don't have as much hard news, so they have more room in their newscasts for soft news, the feature-style friendly, community stories. Still, just as with newspaper editors, you need to convince the news director that something about your production is newsworthy.

If you're shooting for news coverage, you don't need to be as picky about a station's music format as you do with advertising; if something about your production is legitimately news, it's news to everyone.

A news story can be anywhere from thirty seconds to a couple of minutes, depending on how much news the station airs and whether it uses soundbites (short interview clips).

Another way to get your production publicized is through public service announcements (PSAs). A PSA is the radio equivalent of a calendar listing. It gives the who, what, where, why, when, and how much, without getting into any other details.

You don't need to worry about targeting PSAs to a particular station. Every station runs them. Stations typically have a bunch of PSAs in rotation at any given time, usually in a little index card box next to the operating board. When a DJ has a few seconds to kill, she'll grab a PSA out of the box and read it. There's no telling when, or how often, your PSA will get read, but the advantage is that they're free. Stations air them as part of their public service mission.

The *Playlist*

Another way to take advantage of radio is through sponsorship. Radio stations offer a unique form of support that other business donors can't: exposure. If you've identified an ideal radio station in your area—maybe it's the *only* radio station in your area—approach them about being your media sponsor.

Be prepared to sell the station on the advantages of a partnership with you:

- List the station's name and logo prominently in all printed material (newsletters, programs, posters, and even ads)... and, of course, you'll include their name as the tag on the radio spots you run on the station.
- List the station in your top tier of donors.
- Supply tickets the station can give away as prizes to their listeners.
- Reinforce the notion of community service—not just the service the station is doing for your theatre, but the service the

theatre provides to the community through artistic enrichment and the service the station is doing for the community
by promoting that artistic enrichment.

■ Add a link from your website to the station's website. If the station webcasts its programs over the Internet, offer to webcast
them from your site, too, if you can.

■ Give a few tickets for each show to station employees. If they
attend, they're likely to talk about the show on the air, before
and after the performance.

In return, ask for radio spots, interview opportunities, and ticket
giveaways.

Ideally, you want to form a partnership that lasts the entire season, for several reasons. First, and most immediately, it frees you up
from negotiating a new agreement for each show. Second, it gives
you the chance to build the relationship and get a more accurate
idea of its effectiveness. Third, it cements a relationship with a credible business partner that enhances your reputation and image in
the business community, which can be helpful come fund-raising
time. Finally, in a strong relationship, the station may be able to help
you out with things that you need for a show, such as special sound
effects.

"Trade isn't always a good thing," cautions Marie Costello, who
works as WESB's promotions director. "You don't always get the best
times for your spots; they're usually inserted into the schedule when
there's a free slot here or there. When you buy your spots, you can
pick and choose where you want them to go."

Radio stations sometimes offer special deals for nonprofit groups,
so be sure to ask your sales rep about that possibility. "We do a match,"
Costello says. "The theatre buys $126 worth of spots, we'll match it
with $126 worth of spots for free."

Give It Away, Give It Away, Give It Away, Give It Away Now

Ticket giveaways are a tried-and-true way to get publicity. Giveaways
are especially effective because you essentially get four commercials
every time a station gives away a pair of tickets:

1. "Hey, coming up this hour, we've got a pair of tickets to give away to the Chekoville Community Theatre's upcoming show, *Fences*."
2. "Now it's time to give away those tickets to the Chekoville Community Theatre's upcoming show, the Pulitzer Prize winner, *Fences*."
3. Someone calls up and wins the tickets.
4. "So-and-so just got herself a pair of tickets to the Chekoville Community Theatre's upcoming show, *Fences*. Your chance to win is coming up."

That's an oversimplification, but that's basically how it works. Your theatre gets mentioned, which is good for the big PR picture, and the show gets mentioned, which is good for the immediate PR picture.

I should point out that I specify "a pair" of tickets. I always used to think it was sooo cheesy when people would ask us to give tickets away one at a time. Who goes to see something alone? Practically no one. The idea, of course, is that the winner will bring a date, and the date will buy a ticket. That's just lame. Don't do it. Treat your winners as special guests, not as cash cows.

Most stations like ticket giveaways, but don't be fooled: They know just as well as you do that giving away tickets is lots of free publicity for you. So be gracious about it. Buy some spots (some stations won't do giveaways unless you're also advertising with them). Work out a sponsorship deal. Offer some tickets to the promotions director or the on-air personalities. *Something.* Anything so that you don't look like a vulture trying to take advantage of the station.

On occasion, people win prizes and, for whatever reason, don't pick them up. Make it clear to the station's promotions director that if there are unclaimed tickets, someone from the station is welcome to use them. Don't let them go to waste. Bodies in seats, especially bodies that may give the show free publicity on the air the next day, are better than empty or even resold seats.

Ask the station how many pairs of tickets it would like to give away. Weigh that against what you can afford. For some theatres, attendance isn't an issue, so giving away seats generates word of mouth that exceeds the value of the ticket price. For companies where attendance is an issue, consider how many seats you can afford to give up and weigh that against what the station may ask of you.

Remember, the exchange needs to be worth the station's while as well as the theatre's.

　When you drop tickets off at the station, provide a fact sheet about the show. Make sure it includes all the essential information: who, what, where, when, and how much. You can include other details as well, such as cast members or musical numbers. Just make sure you don't overwhelm the station with info. The fact sheet will then give the DJs something to talk about when they're giving away the tickets (and, if you're lucky, something to talk about even when they're *not* giving away tickets).

　Finally, keep track of the tickets you give to the station so you can see how many of them actually get used. This will help you decide how effective your relationship with the station is.

Things to Think About

- Which radio stations best appeal to your audience?
- Who is best-suited to represent your theatre company in radio interviews?
- Is there a news angle to your show you can use to attract radio coverage?
- If you approach a radio station about media sponsorship, what's in it for the station?
- How many pairs of tickets can your company afford to give away for each performance?

7 TV or Not TV? That Is the Question

TV. I can't think of two other letters that, when combined, say sooo much. It's the good, the bad, and the ugly of our society all rolled into one vacuum tube full of electrons.

It's easy to think of TV as the antithesis of theatre. TV is one-way, unlike the two-way exchange that takes place between a live audience and actors on stage. TV has virtually no spontaneity. It comes in convenient, easy-to-predict packages. It's passive. It's free. It's in your home. You can sit on your sofa in your underwear, with a beer in one hand and the remote in the other, and have your entertainment spoon-fed to you.

We also think of TV as something big and flashy and expensive. It wows us when we see it happen. One of my best friends is a news anchor for a network affiliate in Bangor, Maine, and when we go out to dinner together, people look at him with awe. They're starstruck. (If only they knew his nickname is Bubba Cheese they'd probably think differently.)

TV is, for the most part, a city thing. A number of small cities, like Bangor; Altoona, Pennsylvania; and Hobbs, New Mexico, have their own stations, but for most small towns, the "local" TV station is in the nearest metro area. For instance, Buffalo is the closest metro area for me, and I live an hour and a half south. To people in my area, the Buffalo newscasters are like old family friends who come into our homes every evening; to the Buffalo news people, we might as well be on the other side of the globe. Imagine trying to persuade them to come down and cover one of the theatre's productions.

So how can we, as Theatre People, use the Dark Powers of Television to our advantage?

The News Hole Can Be Your Friend

When you think of your local TV stations, you probably think of the news people. Most local stations don't generate any other type of programming besides news. Some produce morning talk shows, but those are essentially feature-driven programs, and features are soft news.

In a metro area, there's usually enough hard news to fill a newscast easily. Because there's so much news, and because competition is so tight, stations have a multitude of news programs. Some have morning, 5:00 P.M., 5:30 P.M., 6:00 P.M., and 11:00 P.M. broadcasts; if they have nothing else, they at least have 6:00 and 11:00 P.M. newscasts.

That's a lot of news, right? Don't forget to factor in all the twenty-four-hour cable news channels. We can eat, drink, and sleep TV news if we want.

With all that news available, what makes the local evening news stand out? It's *local*. CNN is not going to tell you what the city council is up to. It's not going to tell you about the fire downtown. It's not going to tell you about the new baby giraffe at the zoo.

Of course, not every day is chock full of politics, disasters, and baby giraffes. Nonetheless, all those news programs still need to show *something*. That's called a news hole: broadcast time (or, in print media, space on a page) that needs to be filled with news.

News is only news when it's new, when it has a huge impact, when it has proximity, or when it has a lot of human-interest potential. There's usually enough good stuff in a typical day to fill the 6:00 P.M. newscast. But once you air something, it's no longer new. Depending on the impact, proximity, and interest, news directors can only recycle a certain amount of that news to fill the 11:00 P.M.

newscast. Likewise, they can only recycle a certain amount from 11:00 P.M. to fill the morning newscast the next day. That means they need to come up with something else to fill that time.

In other words, pray for slow news days. A story that might get covered on a slow day has no chance of getting covered when there's been a triple murder, a tornado downtown, an explosion at the soft-drink bottling plant, or a visit from the pope. When there's nothing exciting going on, assignment editors start paging through their file of potential feature stories.

So, what you want to do is give the assignment editor something to nibble on that can last for a week or two. That way, if you call and make a pitch on a busy day, the story can sit for a few days and not get stale. When that slow news day comes along, your story idea is ready and waiting.

Coverage Options

When you call the newsroom to ask for coverage, ask to speak to the assignment editor. If she isn't available, try the news director. You need to be ready with two things:

- What's your hook? Everything I said about hooking newspaper editors holds true for TV people as well.
- What do you have that'll make good pictures? TV is a visual medium. If you can't provide good pictures, then what's the point?

For instance, A. R. Gurney's *Love Letters,* although a touching and popular play, isn't too dynamic to look at. It doesn't make for good TV pictures. But the physical comedy of *Something Funny Happened on the Way to the Forum* or a swashbuckling swordfight from *Romeo and Juliet* both have plenty of dynamic elements that make for good viewing.

Most often, a news crew that comes to do a story on your production will do a v/o, a voice-over. A photographer will take some pictures and edit them into a twenty- or thirty-second piece, and the newscaster will read a script while the images show on the screen. If you're lucky, you might get a v/o with sound: At a certain point in the script, the newscaster stops talking and the station runs a soundbite in which a spokesperson from your group says something about the show.

If the pope is in your show, or there's some other miracle, the station might do a package. That happens when a reporter shows up with the photographer. The reporter asks questions and then shoots a stand-up, where she stands someplace where there's something going on in the background and delivers a transition or concluding statement. The crew then goes back to the station, the reporter writes a script, the photog edits the tape, and the reporter records the v/o (rather than the newscaster doing it live) and includes the stand-up. During the newscast, the anchor introduces the package with something like "Eyewitness News reporter Dario Fo has the story," and the package airs.

Packages about a community theatre production are rare. Stations save their reporters for hard news stories or fascinating human-interest pieces. If you've got a big, juicy angle, you may get a package, but otherwise, be happy with a v/o with sound.

A Good Rapport

Sam Kuba, whose Theatre Harrisburg (Pennsylvania) offices are conveniently located across the street from ABC affiliate WHTM-TV, has had good luck getting news coverage from the station. "There's a couple reasons for that," he explains. "We have a very good rapport with them."

One of the secrets, says Kuba, is comp tickets. "The deal is sort of 'Hey, if any of you guys want tickets for anything, or anytime you just want to come, just give me a call. We'll take care of you.' And we always take care of things," Kuba says. "That's the part of the bargain, though. When you say that, then when they call, you take care of them."

Some staffers at the theatre initially had doubts about Kuba's freewheeling comp-ticket policy. "But you know what? We found the more tickets I gave away, the more our overall ticket sales went up," he says.

"So when the news director at WHTM calls me up and says 'Sam, I'd really like to see this show. Can you get me tickets for Saturday night?' I say 'Of course.' And I take them over and drop them off," Kuba says. "Then, conversely, when a show's not selling well I call him up and say, 'You know, it would be great if you could do some sort of little feature on the show. We're just not moving the tickets the way we'd like to. Do you think there's anything you could do for me?' " The result, of course, is that the station sends a camera crew to rehearsal to shoot something for the 11:00 P.M. broadcast.

Other theatres in the same media market don't have the same luck, nor does Theatre Harrisburg have the same kind of luck with the other network affiliates (and the CBS affiliate, WHP-TV, is right next door). "We don't get a whole lot of attention from TV," admits Erica Carl of the Little Theatre of Mechanicsburg, in a suburb of Harrisburg. "We had a feature on one of the stations for a recent production of *Scrooge,* but that's been about it."

The NBC affiliate in the Harrisburg media market, WGAL, is based in nearby Lancaster, Pennsylvania, which is also home to the Fulton Opera House. "They will give us coverage on certain things," says Patricia Fackler, the Fulton's director of marketing and public relations. But WGAL's primary relationship with the theatre centers around a specific event. "They have been the media sponsor for more than a decade for our holiday show, as their gift to the theatre," says Fackler. "They usually film a television commercial for us for that show specifically. That has worked out well, and it's something they look at as part of their plan."

WGAL also works with the Fulton on the opera house's Women Who Care awards. WGAL's female anchor serves as the honorary chair of the awards committee. "She gives us a great deal of coverage for that program, which is usually wrapped around a show," Fackler says.

I'll be honest: Coverage from TV news is a rare thing. But that doesn't mean you can't give it a try. The number one rule is, don't be intimidated. It's easy to get that starstruck feeling, and some TV people even try to cultivate it. But they breathe the same air as the rest of us. The worst they can do is say no (and make you feel three inches tall for asking), but remember: All they're doing is TV; we, as Theatre People, do magic.

It's Cheaper than You Think (The Secret of Cable TV Advertising)

Fortunately, TV offers avenues for exposure aside from traditional broadcast news.

Since the early 1980s, cable TV has exploded, bringing more channels to more people in more areas. Gone are the days of the Big Three networks. Now you can surf through hundreds of specialized cable channels that appeal to highly targeted audiences.

Here again, knowing your audience can pay off. If you have a demographic profile of your audience, you can reach the right demographic groups through the types of cable TV programs they watch. For example, a look at the three most popular cable channels for advertisers shows some important demographic info. (These statistics come from Adelphia Media Services. You can get similar information from your local cable sales representative.)

A&E   Adults 25 +

A&E is a leader in delivering upscale working women, and it attracts audiences that spend big dollars on high quality goods and services. It's "where smart money spends its time."

Lifetime   Women 25 +

Lifetime is the highest-rated network for women 18–49.

ESPN   Men 18 +

ESPN delivers more men 18 +, men 18–34, men 18–49, and men 25–54 with annual household incomes exceeding seventy-five thousand dollars than any other cable network does.

"Cable doesn't just reach the general public, it reaches specific audiences," says Myra Neefe, who's with the office of media development for Adelphia Communications, one of the nation's largest cable TV providers. "If you want a category of people, we can specifically target them and pinpoint which channels to advertise on and at what times. That's the beauty of it."

In most cases, a sales representative from your local cable company can help you effectively choose the channels that best match the profiles of your audience. Of course, the better you know your audience, the better your sales rep can help you find the right times and channels to run your ads.

Because we perceive television as something expensive and glitzy, many people tend to write it off as an advertising possibility. But, to quote the great TV sage Bart Simpson, "Au contraire, mon frère."

"Most people have no idea how much a few hundred dollars will buy them on television," Neefe says. "In most cases, it's a lot more affordable than newspapers. And a cable ad gives you sight *and* sound."

Production costs for a spot aren't all that high, either, although they vary from market to market. Once you have a spot made, you can edit it to be play-specific if you want. By simply changing the "supers" (the text in a commercial that's superimposed on the video), you can update the show title, dates, and ticket information from production to production.

There's one other place to consider for TV advertising. Ever watch the Weather Channel? It posts local weather at the "eights" (eight minutes past, eighteen minutes past, etc.). Most cable companies run a message beneath the weather conditions, crawling along the bottom edge of the screen. That space, the "weather crawl," is generally for sale.

Free TV

Another of the beauties of television is public access TV. To ensure the open exchange of ideas and as an anti-monopoly tactic, the federal government mandates all cable companies to provide the public with free access, which usually takes the form of a "message channel." Groups are permitted to submit public service announcements (PSAs), which then air on one of the channels that come with the basic cable subscription package. There's usually music or a local radio station playing in the background, and message after message flashes across the screen.

Do not underestimate the number of people who watch the message channel. You'd be surprised. For some, it's the primary way of keeping up-to-date with events in the community. Others have it on just so there's noise in the room.

It's easy to forget about the local message channel, but look at it this way: It's free, using it takes little effort, and it reaches a large audience (most of whom need something to do—why else would they be sitting at home, watching the message channel?).

Each cable system is slightly different, so check with the local cable office to find out the procedure for submitting information.

Most have a form that takes about two minutes to fill out. Some will let you take a stack of forms. Others will let you turn in an entire season's worth of forms at once and will keep them on file until the appropriate air time.

Some cable systems provide public access opportunities beyond simple message channels, airing locally produced programs that cover a variety of interests. The programs are usually hosted by someone who has a vested interest in the subject matter. For instance, the director of the local Humane Society might have a weekly show that features animals up for adoption. Likewise, the local arts council might have a show that features area arts events. If there's not a specific show focusing on the arts, there might be one that's general enough to include your group's activities.

"Our local cable TV has a local show, *CableTalk*, that runs fifteen minutes a day," says Richard Bennett, president of the Little Theatre of Winchester (Virginia). "The host is a local radio personality who goes on the TV and interviews local people doing local things. We try to get on that when we can find interested people to do it. We tape it a week before [opening night] and it shows somewhere close to opening night."

If your public access channel airs locally produced shows, you might contact the cable system's office to inquire about the possibility of creating a show that focuses on the arts. Typically, the system provides the crew; you would provide the host and the guest. Just remember, it can be tough to sustain such a show. However, it might make an exciting joint venture for arts groups in your area to collaborate on.

Things to Think About

- If you're calling a TV assignment editor, what's your hook? What will make for good pictures?
- Which cable channel's demographics match up best with your audience demographics?
- What is the procedure for submitting a PSA to the local message channel?
- What other public access features does your local cable channel offer?

8 The World Wide Whatsit? (And Why It's So Important)

I recently surveyed hundreds of community theatres across the country and was amazed to discover how few of them have websites. Many theatres had sites "in progress" or "under construction," but a majority of the companies who responded didn't have a site up and running.

That's understandable, I guess. After all, our first love, as Theatre People, is, well ... theatre. If we were techies, we would all work for Bill Gates. But what I found ironic is the vast majority of people who responded to the survey included an email address.

Yep, Theatre People use email. They use the Internet. They use the Web. Surprise, surprise, eh? But ... if you assume that you, as a Theatre Person, bear at least some resemblance to your audience, you can assume many of your audience members use the Web, too.

So why wouldn't your theatre have a webpage? I've heard three common arguments:

1. We don't need one.
2. It costs too much.
3. It's too complicated.

And, of course, I have simple answers for each argument:

1. Yes you do.
2. No it doesn't.
3. No it's not.

We could do this the easy way—you could just take my word on those points—but you paid good money for this book and you're expecting explanations, so here I go . . .

Yes, You Need a Website (Or, What Your Website Says About Your Theatre)

Your theatre needs a website because most people expect you to have one. It's that simple. This is the Digital Age . . . the Information Age . . . the Age of Convenience . . . whatever. Websites meet the needs of all three.

The Web is today's fastest-growing medium. Everyone and his uncle and kid sister can put up a website—and most do. Every self-respecting business has a website, and some businesses do *billions* of dollars of business via the Web.

What's especially important is that the Web is a controlled medium. *You* control it. You control the content. You control how and when it's presented. You control the message.

You also get to go more in-depth with information that you wouldn't have time enough to include in a radio PSA or space enough to include in a newspaper ad. Someone who's heard that PSA or seen a poster or heard a tip from a friend can look up information about a particular show online. While they're at it, they get your cyber sales pitch.

Your website is available twenty-four/seven. You don't have to depend on media gatekeepers, news holes, or even the postal service. You do have to depend on a Web provider, but service providers make their money by being dependable.

Aside from providing information to your audience, a website also sends a message about the kind of organization you are. That's important not only for potential audience members but also for potential donors, particularly business and corporate givers. Are you a modern organization, or are you behind the times? Do you have exciting things to say, or are you cyber-silent?

Can you be counted among the members of the local online community, with links from the chamber of commerce, schools and colleges, the tourism bureau, and the arts council . . . or are you a nonentity? A website allows you to link to and from these entities, which almost certainly all have websites of their own. An online presence proves your theatre is a vital, integral part of the community. That presence, regardless of your actual site, creates a specific perception that works in your favor (and remember the old adage about truth being four-fifths perception?).

So, yes, you need a website.

No, It Doesn't Cost Too Much (Or, Think Resource, Not Revenue Source)

Many people assume that if it's technology, it must be expensive. If it's *new* technology then, yes, it's expensive. Remember when camcorders were a thousand bucks? Now they're a couple hundred. The Web is the same way. The technology has gotten cheaper as it's gotten better. Competition has gotten stiffer, too, which helped bring the cost down.

If you look around, you should be able to find a company that can host your website for three or four hundred dollars a year. Most offer payment plans and technical support. They can even register your site and help secure a domain name for you (www.this_is_the_domain_name.com).

One crucial thing to keep in mind, though: Price is not the only factor to consider when choosing an Internet service provider (ISP). You need to also look at the amount of space it offers, whether you get any email addresses to go along with your space, what sort of technical work the ISP can do for you, and what technical support it can offer. Do not fail to consider these factors: It will save you headaches later!

Mary Jean McDonald, a producer with the Puget Sound Musical Theatre in Des Moines, Washington <*www.psmt.org*>, says their theatre's webmaster has been extremely accommodating. "We have a phenomenal young man responsible for all that beautiful work, and he so far has charged what we can afford," she says.

Will your theatre's website pay for itself through ticket sales? Some theatres sell tickets via the Web, so literally, the site pays for itself. But even if you can't or don't want to do Web sales, the site can still generate money for you as a development tool because you can point potential donors to your site for all the information they want about your theatre.

If you're really interested in making money via the Web, the online superstore Amazon.com offers fund-raising opportunities through its Associates Program. Your theatre puts a link to Amazon.com on its page. If shoppers go to Amazon through that link and make a purchase, a portion of the proceeds go back to the theatre as a "referral fee." A complete description of the program can be found at <www.amazon.com/associates>.

However, the smartest way to look at your website is as a resource rather than as a revenue source. It's not there to generate money; it's there to inform your audience. An informed audience translates into dollars because an informed audience member is a lot more likely to buy a ticket than someone who's uninformed.

So, no, a website does not cost too much.

No, It's Not Too Complicated (Yes, It's Easier than You Think)

Just as the technology has gotten cheaper, it has also gotten easier to use. Remember what I said just a few paragraphs ago about the kid sister? I wasn't exaggerating.

Scott Bloom, webmaster for The Theatre Pages, says people get way too intimidated: "A lot of them have the same situation—that someone's friend or son/daughter or a peripheral member of the group has done the website, and they're afraid if they lose that connection they won't know how to continue to maintain the site. And they tell me that the site doesn't get updated regularly because it's a low priority for the person doing it."

The Theatre Pages <www.srbnet.com> hosts sites for nearly one hundred community theatres in Maryland, Virginia, and Washington, D.C. The site also offers resource materials and tips on website upkeep. "A lot of groups need some kind of basic instruction that anyone can follow about how to maintain and update the site themselves," Bloom says.

Fortunately, most Web browsers, including Netscape and Microsoft Explorer, come with their own tools that allow you to create webpages on your own computer. The programs are easy to learn, and they make it simple to manipulate colors and text, add graphics, and create tables to align your information. Just a few hours of playing around will turn you into a webpage-creating whiz.

If you want more bells and whistles on your page, such as Javascript or Flash or audio or video files, the software isn't too expensive. If you don't want to make the investment, you might find a bored high school or college kid who already has the software and is willing to do a little freelance work for you at a low cost (maybe even in exchange for tickets).

Your Web host might also offer tech support to help you do some of the more intricate stuff. Your ISP's tech support is incredibly important.

So, obviously, the Web is not too complicated.

Don't Be e-Timidated

I've included the Web here, in the mass-media section of this book, because it has the potential to reach huge audiences. But this discussion also serves as a good transition into the next section of the book, which deals primarily with controlled media. The Web gives you the advantages of both uncontrolled, mass media (large audience numbers) and smaller, controlled media (control of the message).

Because of the Web's convenience and accessibility and your ability to control the message, you should promote your website as the number one source of information about your theatre. Plaster that Web address on everything: Stationery. Business cards. Newsletters. Postcards. Posters. Refrigerator magnets. Everywhere you can think of. *If it has your phone number on it, it should have your Web address on it, too.*

Why? The phone requires someone to be at the other end of the line, and there are certain times of day when it's not cool to call—I hate those 2:00 A.M. calls about ticket prices, don't you? A website is available at the user's convenience.

Let me put it into a different context: *If you don't yet have a website, it should immediately become your number one priority.* Get a website up, even if you have to start basic and expand from there.

Treat your website like any other publication you produce. Make sure its look is consistent with your other materials (something we'll touch on in more depth in Chapter 9). Make sure the site is accurate and up-to-date, professional looking, and easy to read. And don't forget: Proofread, proofread, proofread.

Making a Splash

When someone types in your domain name and your webpage pops up, the first thing they see is the splash page, also known as the index page. It's called a splash page because it's the first thing that splashes on screen, and it needs to make the right kind of splash.

The splash page sets the tone for the entire site, and it should embody the things that make up your theatre company's identity. Are you a formal, traditional theatre? Then your splash page should have a formal, traditional look with subdued colors and small to medium-sized pictures. Are you a jazzy theatre? Then your splash page should jump off the screen with an exciting look. Whatever look you choose, just make sure it's consistent with the theatre's identity. For instance, when most people see Shakespeare, they think "theatre." But don't put Willy's picture on your website if you don't do his plays.

A good splash page has several other features:

- *Your name.* Sounds obvious, right? You'd be surprised . . . Get your name right up there at the top, in an easy-to-see spot. Don't let it get lost in visual clutter.
- *Your logo.* Don't make it huge, but get it on there, toward the top if possible. Your logo is an important part of your branding (which we'll address in Chapter 9).
- *Pictures.* The Web is a visual medium, so pictures are a must. Don't make them big because big pictures take forever to download. On the splash page, you want three or four. You can also incorporate them into a slide show so they flash on screen in a sequence.

- *A welcoming statement.* Too often, I've looked at sites that have the theatre's name, maybe a logo or a picture, and then a list of links. Don't forget your manners! Welcome people to your site. The welcoming statement can include a number of things. Backstage Theatre, Inc. *<www.backstagetheatre.org>* in Breckenridge, Colorado, keeps it short and sweet:

> Backstage Theatre has been presenting award-winning the-atre since 1974. Join us this season as we present a series of terrific shows! An evening at Backstage is an evening of memorable live entertainment, presented in a warm and cozy atmosphere, and sure to be the highlight of your day. Shows sell out quickly, so don't hesitate—call now for reser-vations. Let us carry you away for an evening of fantastic, live theatre.

- The Imagination Theater *<www.imagination-theater.org>* in Placerville, California, is more detailed:

> You know IT when you see IT! That is the aim of Imagination Theater. We are a nonprofit community theater company, located in Placerville, CA. We strive to "Tell good stories well in an atmosphere of respect, trust, challenge, personal growth and integrity."
>
> IT was established in 1999 to provide a professionally administered, creative youth and family-oriented perform-ing arts company.
>
> With the upcoming production of *Alice in Wonderland,* and auditions for *Sound of Music,* following the 13 sold-out performances of *Grease,* we have met our original goal to produce 2 major shows a year by 2001.
>
> Find out more about IT! Click on the navigation bar at the top left of your screen.
>
> For show and ticket information, call the Imagination Theater information line.

Whatever your approach, remember that the text helps set the tone, so make sure it sets the *right* tone.

- *Navigation bar.* Most successful sites I've visited arrange their list of links along the left side of the page. Each link takes you to a page or pages with relevant information. We'll talk more about links in a sec.

- *Contact information.* At the bottom of the splash page—in fact, at the bottom of every page—include an email address or phone number so people can get in touch with you if they have questions or want to order tickets. Make it as easy as possible for them to find your contact info. Your splash page should also have your mailing address, or an easy-to-identify link to a page that has your mailing address.

One other important note: Text-heavy pages are a no-no. They're unattractive and hard to read.

Organizing Your Website

Once you've given thought to the splash page, you want to start mapping out the rest of the site. What information do you want on the site? Who will use the site?

One unique feature of the Web is that the user has the ability to define herself and then seek information relevant to that identity. In other words, a hopeful actor seeking audition information is different from a prospective donor, who is different from someone who performed with you several seasons ago and has since moved away but is surfing through your site to relive the good old days. And there's also that person looking for show information because she may want to buy a ticket to the upcoming production.

In each case, the user wants information that's not necessarily of interest to other types of users. The pages you create within your website must keep many audiences in mind.

Let me offer one word of caution: Plan the website carefully because too many links can create clutter on the navigation bar and make it tough to use your site.

Your site's pages will, of course, be specific to your theatre's needs. Some things you might include:

- archives (past newsletters, info about past shows, scanned news clippings, etc.)
- audition info (when, where, and available parts)
- company history
- directions (where you are and how people can get there)
- links (theatre-related sites and resources on the Web, points

of interest in town, arts organizations, websites of company members)

- mission statement (what the theatre stands for)
- personnel info (board members, paid staff people, key volunteers)
- the season (upcoming productions, including titles, dates, and times)
- sponsors (another way to recognize donors for their gifts!)
- submission guidelines (if you accept original scripts from playwrights)
- ticket purchase information

Perhaps you want to include information about special services your theatre offers. For instance, the Reading Community Players (Pennsylvania) provides services to the hearing impaired. The theatre received a grant that pays for a sign language interpreter for one performance during each run of a show. The website provides details about which performances are signed.

I've arranged the above suggestions in alphabetical order just for your convenience. Links on your webpage should be organized in a way that caters to the various audiences who'll be using the page. For instance, board of directors members might feel mighty pleased if the link to their page is at the top of the list—after all, they're the board, right?—but are people really coming to the site to find out about the board? Aren't more people coming to find out about the next show? Always keep your audiences in mind when putting the webpage together.

Design of the Times

Aside from content, you also need to look at design. The number one rule: Just because you *can* do something doesn't mean you *should* do it.

Just because you can animate all your titles so they jump around and do groovy little dances doesn't mean you should (the text will be hard to read). Just because you can do a slide show with ten giant pictures doesn't mean you should (it'll take forever to download). Just because you can toss in all sorts of bright, splashy colors doesn't mean you should (one word: eyestrain). Just because you can use frames doesn't mean you should (not all browsers can view frames, and not all composing programs can edit frames).

In that context, there are several important design points to keep in mind:

- *Do the pages all look like they belong to the same website?* Consistency within the site is important in order to reinforce your image. It also keeps your audience from getting confused. For instance, just because you can add all sorts of interesting fonts doesn't mean you should. It gets confusing and quickly becomes obvious that you're switching fonts simply for the sake of switching fonts.

  A popular technological trick that promotes consistency is the use of frames, which keep the navigation bar the same but let a user jump from page to page inside an onscreen window. It's a sort of shortcut, but I recommend against frames because, from a technological point of view, they require a level of skill most Web novices don't have. That means the number of people who can maintain your site is pretty limited. The simpler you keep the technology, the more people in your company will be able to learn how to maintain your site and create pages if the need ever arises. (Not to mention the fact that not many people have the technology to do frames.)

  Instead of frames, I create a template based on the splash page. This will enable you to keep your name, logo, and navigation bar in the same place on each page throughout the site. It also creates consistency with fonts and colors.

  And don't forget, always put contact info at the bottom of each page.
- *Is your website easy to navigate?* Can you get around within the site, not just from the splash page into the site but from interior page to interior page? Make sure not only that the navigation bar stays in the same place, but also that the navigation buttons remain consistent. If you need to add new links, do so in a spot away from the main navigation bar. If you have someone who knows Javascript, she can create pop-up submenus from your main buttons.
- *Is the site easy on the eyes?* Make the site visually appealing, not busy or gaudy. For instance, don't go overboard on color. Most colored backgrounds make text tough to read. Likewise,

colored fonts can be hard to read. Have you ever tried to read red text on a black backround? Make your color choices carefully and with purpose. Colors should be complementary, not contrasting. Don't make the theatre's name one color, the title of each show a different color, and photo captions yet another color, all on a soft pink background. I strongly recommend a white background with one or two colors for headlines and a nice dark color (usually black) for text.

Also, the size of your text can affect its readability. A 10-point font is pushing the lower limits; I'd recommend a 12-point font just to be safe. Remember, resolution on a computer monitor isn't nearly as sharp as print resolution. The standard computer screen only lets you look at 72 dpi (dots per inch), although a few monitors have slightly higher resolution. That low resolution makes it tough to see subtle details, so when you shrink fonts too small, they get hard to read, particularly for the elderly.

- *How do the pictures look?* Scan pictures at a resolution of 72 dpi, because that's the standard monitor resolution. I usually scan at 100 dpi so I can catch those few monitors with slightly sharper resolution, but if you scan at a resolution any higher than that, you create bigger files, which take longer to download— and the picture that shows up on the screen doesn't look any sharper because the monitors are still only 72 dpi, anyway. True, pictures scanned at 100 dpi are not suitable for downloading and printing, but I recommend against that anyway. (Print from original photos whenever possible.)

If you scan a picture in at a width of 200 pixels, then try to stretch the picture to something like 250 pixels, the picture will look terrible. On the other hand, you can shrink without sacrificing resolution. That's why I always scan at a slightly larger size than I think I'll need—I can always shrink the picture, but I can't expand it.

What Tangled Webs We Weave

So you pour all this effort into a website. Then what?

You want people to keep visiting the site, so put information there that will be of use to them. Most importantly, keep your information up to date. Nothing turns people off more than going to a site and finding information from two shows ago and a banner that says "Coming Soon!" People will stop visiting.

Don't get into the mindset that you have to build the site around your shows, either. If you have downtime between productions, use the website to promote your special events, giving opportunities, plans, and anything else you can think of to keep the content fresh.

Erie Playhouse in Erie, Pennsylvania, gets people to revisit its site with a weekly quiz. "The purpose," says marketing director Sue Lechner, "was to get people to our website and involved in our 2001–02 season. All the answers to the quiz questions are somewhere on our website, and they all relate to the new season."

In the quiz's first week, eleven people responded. But it wasn't long before the number of respondents grew. "I placed inserts in our playbills and have blurbs in our ads, both print and electronic, alerting people to the quiz," Lechner says. By week two, responses had doubled, and in subsequent weeks they climbed at a steady rate, "not in leaps and bounds," Lechner points out. Weekly winners receive a pair of tickets to a mainstage show; the grand prize winner captures a "super family pack" with four season tickets.

Not only did Lechner achieve her goal of attracting people to the website with the quiz, she also accomplished something else. "I'm trying to find ways to reach that younger segment of the ticket-buying population as opposed to our over-fifty regular customers," she explains. The quiz has helped her tap into that new demographic.

The Web offers so many possibilities as a PR tool. Don't let them go to waste. Use the Web to get the word out about the magic you do.

Things to Think about

- If you don't have a website, why not?
- What would it take for you to have a website up and running in three months?
- What Web support services do local Internet providers offer?
- On what materials is your Web address printed? Where else can you put it so people will see it?

- What do you want your website to say about the theatre?
- What audiences will use your website?
- How can you tailor the content of your website to accommodate the different groups of people who'll visit it?
- What resources, including links, do you want to make available through your website?

9 You've Got the Look (And Everything You Do Should, Too)

A theatre company down south (which shall remain nameless for reasons that will soon become apparent) recently showed off its new logo to me.

"I hate it," said the managing director. "We all hate it. Everyone here on staff. Most of the board does, too."

I took another look at the logo. I could see a vague resemblance to an albatross.

"We're stuck with it," said the managing director. "When you set the rules and make them public, you've got to play by them."

The theatre had decided on a logo redesign as part of its anniversary season, and thought it would generate good press to hold a logo contest. The theatre selected three prominent community members to serve as judges, and this panel would choose, from the entries, the new logo. The winning logo would become the full and complete property of the theatre, no strings attached.

Dozens of entries poured in, ranging from sketches drawn by kids to projects drafted by college design students to submissions crafted by graphic arts firms. As the theatre had hoped, the contest drew a lot of press coverage. The media were invited to attend the logo unveiling, where the winning design was shown to the board of directors for the very first time.

Nobody loved the winner.

"Maybe 'hate' is too strong of a word," said the managing director. "But aside from the judges, no one was wild about it. It was just like 'Oh. Hmm. Well.'"

That put the theatre in a difficult situation. It had generated a massive amount of hype, and it didn't give itself any safety valves. So, what it ended up with was an abstract three-color design that looks nice but says nothing about the theatre or the city it's in.

"I'm trying to think of ways to use it really small," the managing director explained. "We're already over-logoed as it is. This is just one more." He showed me the theatre's latest direct-mail piece, adorned with logos for the state theatre association, the national theatre association, the local arts council/funding agency, the state council for the arts, and the theatre's media sponsor. "I just chucked our logo down there with the rest of them."

On the direct-mail piece, in full color, the logo looked busy. But on the managing director's business card, printed in only two colors, it looked much better.

"We're going with it. We have no choice," said the managing director. "We'll see what happens."

Logomania

Living with an ugly logo is like living with a big wet dog: It stinks.

Your logo simply *must* go on everything you print or publish because it's a readily recognizable symbol that represents who you are. It creates a first impression that sets the tone for how you want people to perceive the theatre. To do so, it needs to stand out, not get buried in clutter.

Nearly every theatre company has a logo, but there are some that don't. If you don't have one, get one. If you do have one, make sure it's doing the right job for you. Some things to consider when looking at your logo:

- It should, obviously, be attractive (although that's a highly subjective criterion).

- It should be easy to recognize. It shouldn't be something folks will find confusing.
- It should look as good in color as it does in black-and-white.
- It should say something about the organization. It could also say something about the theatre's location. For instance, the Island Players of Washington Island, Wisconsin, use a large "i.p." for a logo, with the dot on the "i" shaped like a silhouette of Washington Island. The logo of the Puget Sound Musical Theatre in Des Moines, Washington, has musical notes descending from a music staff that runs beneath an image of Mount Olympus.

- Got a building? That's what The Spirit of Broadway Theater in Norwich, Connecticut, uses as the main element in its logo. The logo has two configurations, depending on where it's being used.

- Many theatres use their name as a logo. How much more recognizable can your logo get? Longmont (Colorado) Theatre Company uses contrasting typefaces, with "Theatre" in a red script splashed across "Longmont" and "Company" in a tall, thin roman typeface.

- Some theatres use their initials. Windsor (Colorado) Community Playhouse uses a fun font and a pair of theatre masks as a logo.
- Finally, and most practically, the logo should be clear when it's printed small. I've seen instances where someone has designed a gorgeous logo, but when it got printed on a business card or piece of letterhead, all the fine detail got lost and the logo looked like a cloudy mess. Test your logo at different sizes before you get married to a design.

When you have a logo you're happy with, plaster it all over everything. After all, what good is a logo if you don't use it? I have seen newsletters, brochures, and even advertisements with no logo. That's a no-no. Use that logo. It is the most important component of your theatre's image.

Look Good/Do Good

Why is image important? I had a fraternity brother once tell me "Look good, do good." Poor grammar, but good advice. If you look spiffy and professional, you're more apt to act that way. That's also how people will treat you. So much of who we are as theatres (heck, as people) consists of who we are to others—our volunteers, our patrons, our performers and techies, and, most importantly, our audience.

Therefore, it's important to decide on what you want the theatre's image to be. What do you want people to think of when they hear the theatre's name or see its logo?

Once you have that down, everything you do as a theatre company, and particularly as a PR person, should cultivate and reinforce that image.

For instance, Theatre Jacksonville in Florida is one of the oldest continuously operating community theatres in the country. What does it cultivate as its image? The theatre's age—and the experience and the level of quality implied by that. On everything it sends out, it prints

Theatre Jacksonville
Since 1919

Use everything at your disposal: slogans; the standard paragraph in your news releases; the layout and design of your publications; color selections; photos. Even consider the typeface you print your name in. For instance,

Gurney Little Theatre

certainly has a different look from

Gurney Little Theatre

or

G·u·r·n·e·y L·i·t·t·l·e T·h·e·a·t·r·e

StageWest in Des Moines, Iowa, promotes itself as "Just slightly off-center and way west of Off-Broadway." If you're a Theatre Person, you have a pretty good idea of what that slogan implies; if you're not, it still sounds offbeat and fun. But StageWest doesn't stop there. Its brochure uses language that reinforces its off-center image: "sometimes irreverent, occasionally shocking, always invigorating, rejuvenate your senses!" To top it off, it uses two contrasting typefaces that really emphasize the image: Times for regular text and a bold postmodern-looking typeface for headlines.

Every choice you make needs to be deliberate, just as if you were on stage. We'll talk more about those choices and the effects they have in subsequent chapters. But however you choose to express your image, you need to run with it.

Look, Image, and Brand, Esq.

Think for a moment about examples from the media. When I say *Time* magazine, what do you think of? Red letters and red border? *National Geographic?* Yellow border. CBS television? The eye logo. Certainly you recognize NBC's peacock. Each of these examples illustrates a well-established and widely recognized look.

You want to achieve a look with your theatre's materials so people can pick up any of your publications or see one of your ads and know it belongs to you without searching all over the place for the theatre's name or without even having to read the piece. When you establish a look, people can immediately recognize something that's yours.

Look—that is, physical appearance—is an important component of *image,* which ties into our general impressions about something. For instance, *USA Today* uses its color as a cornerstone of its look. It also uses splashy design, lots of pictures, and a high story count (more shorter stories rather than fewer longer stories). These things create a particular image for the paper that's quite distinct from, say, the *Wall Street Journal,* which has few pictures, lots of in-depth reporting, and a text-heavy layout. Each paper has a distinctive look that relates to its overall image.

Uniqueness is something you want to capture in your theatre's image. It's what sets you apart. It's what makes your theatre different from anyone and everything else. It's what the marketing people call a *brand*: the association of your name with a product.

In some instances, branding can be too successful. How many times have you asked for a Band-Aid or a Kleenex or Wite-Out, when really all you want is a bandage, a tissue, or correction fluid? These brand names have become so associated with the products that they've become almost universal, and the manufacturers actually have to defend their brand names for copyright purposes. As a result, the cute kids in the commercials are now "stuck on Band-Aid *brand* because Band-Aid *brand's* stuck on me." (Doesn't have quite the same ring, does it?)

By creating a successful brand, you can use your good name—your reputation and your image—as an effective promotional tool.

This brings us to the realm of controlled media. Your image is yours to control through the various publications, articles, photos, and displays your theatre company produces. You can also control your image through any advertisements you buy (although I have, alas, seen advertising gone wrong).

Don't, like the hapless community theatre I mentioned earlier, give up control of your image. Be the master of your destiny. Pick an image that's right for you and make it work.

As a side note: I spoke with a theatre that conducted a similar logo contest . . . except in their case, a panel of five judges picked three finalists, and the board privately chose the winner from that narrowed-down pool. That was a *much* safer approach.

Show and Look

Just as your theatre has a consistent look, your season should have its own look (we'll talk more about that in the next chapter). Likewise, each show should have a look that remains consistent in all of the show's publicity. This is most easily accomplished by turning the show's name into artwork. I call this a title design. You can create a title design by the simple use of distinctive fonts, or a designer can do something really fancy. A well-known example is *Little Shop of Horrors,* with blood dripping from the word "Horrors." Another is *A Chorus Line,* which has distinctive Broadway lights inside the letters of the title. Other examples of title designs can be seen in the newsletter samples in the Appendix.

Whenever you promote the show, make sure to use its title de-sign. Use it in your season brochure, website, newsletter, posters, postcards, print ads, displays, programs, and anywhere else you can. (Obviously, in press releases you would not use the title design.)

You can also go one step further and have artwork created for each show. Use this artwork the same way you'd use title design, and with the same consistency. Don't use different art in different places.

As you read the next few chapters, keep in mind how each aspect of your controlled media can reflect and reinforce your theatre's image and the image of its shows. Make sure everything has The Look.

Things to Think About

- Where do you use your logo? Where else could you be using it?
- What is your theatre's image?
- What unique facet of your theatre is captured in its image?
- Can you pick up one of your theatre's publications and tell that it belongs to your theatre?
- What distinctive look do your publications have?

⬛1⬤ Your Season Brochure Sets the Tone

The trip from downtown Harrisburg, Pennsylvania, to suburban Mechanicsburg takes about fifteen minutes, depending on traffic. On this particular Wednesday afternoon, traffic was light as we headed west across the Susquehanna River. I was riding with Erica Carl, president of the Little Theatre of Mechanicsburg, who was taking me for a tour of the theatre. As we drove, sunroof open, she mentioned she'd soon begin work on a new season brochure—a task she didn't relish.

"Let's whip one together right now," I suggested. Erica laughed. I smiled. She thought I was joking.

"What sort of theme do you have? Any sort of message or something you want to send?" I asked.

"We usually do some variation on our initials, LTM: Live Theatre Magic," she said.

"Magic . . . magic . . . that's good. We can do magic," I said, tossing the idea around in my head for size. "I noticed last year's brochure was three colors because you used that gold foil highlighting along with the black and maroon."

"For our fiftieth anniversary," Erica explained.

"So we'll do two colors this year, unless you're doing a big, splashy fifty-first anniversary celebration. Are you?"

"No," she smirked.

"You want that same kind of glossy white paper stock? Give it that slick feel?"

"Okay." Erica chuckled and nodded. She was realizing I hadn't been joking after all.

"How many shows do you do? Seven? And there's a letter from the president, and a reply coupon and something about ticket info and stuff like that . . . "

"And a mailing panel," she chipped in.

"And a mailing panel. Okay." I did some figuring. "I think we can do all that in eight panels. We'll have to see. You've got a cover, a mailing panel . . . that takes us down to six . . . yeah, we should be able to do that."

"Wow," Erica said. "You just designed my brochure."

This story may sound like an oversimplification, but in essence, that's all the time it takes to come up with a brochure if you have the thematic concept already nailed down. You just need to know which elements to piece together and how those pieces will work to create a unified effect. The rest is just legwork . . . writing the copy and laying it out. A good designer can crank out a brochure in just a couple of hours.

Purpose

Step one, of course, is figuring out what you want the brochure to do. In most cases, you want it to spark ticket sales, either through subscriptions or at the door. Everything about the brochure—the way the copy is written and the way the elements are laid out—needs to be geared toward that purpose.

"You really need to know your audience and the specific purpose or function of the piece," says designer Rachel Rogers of the Rachel Rogers Design Group in Utica, New York. "A beautifully designed brochure that doesn't meet the needs of the client and doesn't 'function,' whether it is to promote, inform, etc., is basically a waste of client money."

Hmm. "You really need to know your audience"... where have I heard that before?

Theme

Next, come up with your thematic concept. That takes some brainstorming.

Most places come up with a season and then look for a theme that fits. Sometimes it's a generic theme that could fit almost anything, like "Live Theatre Magic" or "Your Ticket to Excitement." The theme might also be something quite specific to the shows themselves. A season that includes *West Side Story, Driving Miss Daisy,* and *The Diary of Anne Frank* could easily be billed as a season that explores discrimination and prejudice—quite a worthwhile endeavor for a theatre company whose mission is to educate as well as to entertain.

Maybe your artistic director got to pick her favorite shows, and the season could be billed as such. Maybe it's an anniversary season. Maybe you're doing shows that are all Shakespeare-related. If there's an overriding theme that can tie all the shows together, use it. If there's not, come up with one.

Why? Having a theme gives you an organizing principle around which to build the brochure and the specifics of the season's PR plan. Instead of saying "Our next show will be..." you can play it up—and reinforce your message—by saying "The Live Theatre Magic continues in two weeks with..."

The Longmont (Colorado) Theatre Company chose a roadmap theme for its 2000–2001 brochure. The cover has a map and a highway screened in the background. The theatre's name/logo appears against a green highway sign, and a yellow caution sign proclaims "Great Season Ahead." The theme carries throughout the brochure in various ways. One of the shows, for instance, is *Cyrano de Bergerac.* A yellow caution sign on the page shows two crossed rapiers instead of words. For *Cabaret,* the caution sign says "Curves Ahead."

"A theme gives you elements, color, or a style that can tie the brochure or book together, page by page," says Rogers. "However, sometimes using a theme for the sake of a theme may not work.

That becomes cliché or corny and overworked. It can look clownish. That's why you need to be deliberate in your choices."

Even a good theme can feel gimmicky, but your audience members will be able to latch onto that theme as something that's associated with your theatre, and it will catch their attention more easily with each sighting. That's why your season brochure sets the tone for the rest of the season: It introduces the marketing/PR theme you'll use all year long.

Yes, a theme gets old after a while. That's why you should come up with a new one every year. Give them something new to look for—just so long as they have *something* to look for.

Copy

In the introduction I mentioned the necessity of getting a good writer. Here's where it really pays off. A good writer can take your theme and bang out copy that ties into it.

You don't necessarily have to beat people over the head with the concept:

> Our Live Theatre Magic brings Anne Frank back from the dead through her writing in the courageous story . . .

But if there's a natural way to tie the theme in, go for it.

Keep in mind the main purpose of your season brochure: Your copy should be written to sell tickets. Accentuate the positives. Play up the benefits. Stress the unique.

What "must have" information should the brochure include?

- ticket prices and availability
- contact information (phone, email, and Web address)
- ordering information (who to make the check out to, where to send it, etc.)
- dates, times, and locations of shows (sounds obvious, doesn't it? I've seen people forget to put them in . . .)
- subscription benefits
- reservation and exchange policies
- your logo

Most importantly, the text should be engaging. If your brochure isn't engaging, people will think your shows aren't either.

Budget

Don't you just hate to see the word *budget?* But your budget plays an important role in your brochure production because it affects your paper stock, brochure size, number of copies, and how much color you can use.

Some general budget guidelines:

- The more color you use, the more expensive it is.
- The thicker the paper, the more expensive it is.
- The glossier or whiter the paper, the more expensive it is.
- The more you print, the lower the cost per unit usually is. The real costs in a print job come from the setup, not the actual printing. If you're going to pay the setup to print five thousand copies, you'll find that six thousand copies isn't that much more, and the cost per copy will actually be lower. Don't print six thousand just because you can, but if you can find a use for them, go ahead.

"Know your budget," cautions Rachel Rogers. "Don't overdesign for the budget."

I recommend that you figure out how much money you have to spend and how many copies of the brochure you need, then adjust the other elements to fit the financial parameters. You could do it the other way and go whole-hog for what you want, then figure out later how to pay for it, but I always recommend going on the conservative side where money is concerned, particularly for smaller organizations.

Size and Shape

The amount of copy you have will play a role in determining the size of the brochure. Conversely, the size of the brochure may affect the amount of copy you have. Don't be afraid to edit your copy for space considerations, but don't hack out the important stuff. It's better to rethink the size of your brochure than to leave out important information.

Omaha (Nebraska) Community Playhouse had a beautiful full-color brochure for its 2000–2001 season. Folded, it was only three and a half inches wide by seven inches tall. But it unfolded like a road map (in other words, vertically instead of horizontally), opening out into a poster seven inches wide by twenty-one inches tall.

Aardvark Theatre in El Paso, Texas, had a nifty brochure for its 2001–2002 season. Little bigger than a CD cover, the brochure was roughly five and a half inches square and folded out into three sections, offering six panels, including a cover and a mailing panel.

Hand-in-hand with size is shape. One of the nicest looking brochures I've seen came from the Sheboygan (Wisconsin) Theatre Company for its 2001–2002 season. The brochure conformed to a template eight and a half inches tall and three and a half inches wide, but the top was trimmed at a sixty-degree angle so that it came to a point like the top of a white picket fence. Stuck on a rack with brochures for dozens of other area attractions, this brochure, with its pointy top, would definitely stand out from the others.

Trimming like that is called a die cut. Die cuts aren't cheap. But the Sheboygan brochure was also full-color, with lots of great pictures, and it folded out accordion-style to offer seven panels per side. The brochure looked expensive, but it made the theatre look top-notch.

Fold

Take a sheet of paper. Fold it in half. That's a duo-fold—you get two panels per side. If you fold that same sheet of paper in three, you have a tri-fold—three panels per side. You can fold it accordion-style: Bring the top edge down a third of the way in the front and crease the edge, then take the folded edge down in the back to align with the bottom edge and crease again. Or you can fold it "standard" style: Bring the bottom edge a third of the way up the front and crease, then bring the top edge down the front to match the folded edge and crease.

These are the most common types of folds, but you don't necessarily have to let yourself fall into the most obvious folding configurations. It's not that they're bad or not useful—there's a lot to be said about the ease with which people can fold and unfold these kinds of brochures because of their familiar configurations (picture the evil road map–folding experience and you'll know what I mean).

Sometimes, though, you might want something a little different. That's when you can explore other types of folds.

Take a sheet of legal-size paper. Fold the ends in so that they meet in the middle, which will give you a sheet that's eight and a half inches tall with two three-and-a-half-inch wide panels. Now fold it in half so that the creased edges meet. (You can also try this with an eleven-by-seventeen-inch sheet of paper.)

One of my favorite folds uses a sheet of legal-size paper. Fold · and crease it off-center, so that you have a left panel that's five and a half inches wide and a right panel that's eight and a half inches wide. Now take that extra three inches on the right panel and fold it over so that the edges are all flush. That three-inch flat tucks nicely inside the brochure and serves as a good return-mail coupon.

Don't be afraid to experiment. Just keep in mind that the more origami-like your folds, the tougher it will be for people to navigate their way through your brochure. "The way your design works over each fold also gets trickier," says Rogers. "As you open and close your panels, some elements get covered and uncovered, leaving a 'half-message' by accident."

Color

Full-color printing looks—and is—expensive, but it also looks nifty. Color is particularly effective if you're thinking of pictures, especially pictures with lush costumes and sets. Unfortunately, not everyone can afford full-color, but other options exist.

A one-color printed brochure is better quality than a photocopied brochure, but if you're going to the expense of having a brochure printed, pay the extra few bucks to add a second color if at all possible. This is, after all, your season brochure, and it should represent the theatre as well as possible. You might rather spend your money on the shows themselves, but the brochure is a very necessary evil.

A second color should add emphasis, not just be there for the sake of being there. Make sure your color choices don't just look good together, but that they also look good with the paper you've chosen. Reds and oranges are hot, so they can make effective attention-getters if used sparingly—but they can also easily become overwhelming. Blues and greens are softer and can be used in greater amounts.

Something that can help you choose colors is a PMS color wheel. PMS—the Pantone Matching System—is the standard printers follow for ink colors. A PMS color guide is a worthwhile investment if you do much color printing at all. They're available at most office and art supply stores.

One of the best examples I've seen of a good use of color was the Quincy (Illinois) Community Theatre's 2001 brochure, which used a light teal–colored paper. The ink was a dark, almost black teal, screened back in some places to medium and light shades. Black ink was used as a second color. The brochure had six panels per side and was folded accordion-style. As a topper, it was trimmed so that, unfolded, it sloped from four and a half inches high on the left edge to nine and a quarter inches on the right.

The result, when the brochure was folded, was a zig-zag effect on the cover, with the zig-zags alternating between the shades of teal. Each zig or zag contained one word of the phrase "Quincy Community Theatre 2001" in a shade of teal ink that contrasted with the color of the panel. Text on the black and dark teal panels was reversed out so that the light teal paper showed through in the letters. Medium and light teal panels had black ink and reversed-out boxes.

The overall effect had a dark charisma . . . like Dracula. The brochure created a memorable and attractive impression.

Paper

I've already alluded to paper, which is something you should consider when you're picking ink colors. Paper is the hidden factor that can make or break a brochure.

Paper comes in different weights, which are measured in pounds. The lightest grade of paper is writing, followed by text, then cover. For instance, typical copy paper is 20-pound text.

I don't recommend printing brochures on writing-stock paper. It's used primarily for stationery and is too flimsy to hold up well in the mail. Text-stock paper is usually good enough for brochures, although sometimes you may want something heavier. Heavier paper does mean a higher mailing cost for each brochure.

Along with paper stock, you also want to consider the look and feel of the paper itself. Glossy (shiny and smooth) paper looks and is more expensive than nonglossy paper. It creates a slicker look. On the other hand, a nonglossy paper, such as copy paper, can offer a more low-key look. Textured paper creates a more formal look than nontextured paper; it adds a dash of elegance.

Don't limit yourself to white paper, either; a colored paper can give your publication extra zing as long as it complements the design and your image. Be wary of printing a brochure on colored copy paper, though, because it looks amateurish. It creates the impression that you're using colored paper just because it's not white. That's a poor reason to use colored paper. Instead, choose colored paper for effect. For instance, a sepia paper with black ink offers a rustic look that might be appropriate for a converted-barn theatre. This gets back to the *look* we talked about in the last chapter. If you want people to think of yours as a highly polished theatre, don't use hot pink copy paper. If you want people to think of it as your friendly neighborhood theatre, don't print the brochure on an ivory-colored textured paper.

Paper costs have skyrocketed over the past few years, so make sure you talk to your printer about paper choices that work best for your budget and still offer the look you want the brochure to have. Your printer should be able to give you packets of paper samples, which come from the paper companies. Having samples on hand may give you some new ideas.

Graphic Design and Layout

You have a concept. You have text. You have an idea of the overall look you want, including size and colors. Now you need to put it all on paper (or, in today's graphic design world, you need to arrange it all on computer).

Because software has become so user-friendly, nearly anyone can learn to do layout. It's possible to create your brochure using Microsoft Word. You won't get a lot of bells and whistles, but you can do a competent job.

The problem, though, is that you almost need to have bells and whistles to create the right look and get people's attention. It's not enough to just place the copy and graphics on the page in an attractive, clean way: It's gotta have punch. That's the distinction between *layout* and *design*. There's no good way to describe it other than to call it "pizzazz." I know a lot of people who can do layout, but I know very few people who can do design—and nearly all of them are professionals.

Most professionals use either Quark Xpress or PageMaker, although I've known some to use Freehand. None of these software packages are particularly easy to learn, but if you take the time to work with them, you'll figure it out. Trial and error will teach you the layout skills you need; design skills, on the other hand, are much harder to come by.

For that reason, if you can possibly afford it, I recommend farming out your brochure to a real designer, not just someone who knows how to do desktop publishing. You want the brochure to look its best because it sets the tone for the entire season. It's the first impression your subscribers and patrons will have of your theatre.

Most designers will be happy to help you get the right "feel" to your brochure. They can also help you think in new, creative ways. And many designers will take into consideration that you're a nonprofit group and cut you some slack. Talk to the designer and see what sort of deal you can work out—maybe you can even throw in some tickets.

"Also, know the limitations of your printer," says Rachel Rogers. I know a printer who's a whiz with one- and two-color print jobs but whose full-color jobs aren't very strong. "A great design will fall flat with poor printing," Rogers adds. "We all find out the hard way!"

The bottom line: Don't be afraid to get professional help with your brochure. It's the most important publication you'll create during your season, and it's a driving force behind all your other publications.

Distribution

Who gets your season brochure? This is the one instance where a shotgun approach is the best approach to PR. You want to get that brochure out to as many people as possible because you never know who might be interested in walking through the front door of the theatre to see a show.

You probably have a pretty good idea of who the core of your distribution network is. Like most theatres, you've probably generated a mailing list over the years that consists of patrons, former patrons, folks who regularly come to see one or two shows a season, former actors and techies, volunteers, and so on.

Don't just think "mailing list," though. You can also distribute your brochures in other ways. Send a stack to service groups like the Rotary and Kiwanis Clubs and ask someone to distribute them to all the members. Leave a stack at the library and the chamber of commerce. Of course, keep a stack handy at the theatre where theatregoers can pick one up.

It's always a good thing to have some extra brochures, too, just in case. Order a couple hundred more than you think you'll need. That way, you have some on hand if people request them out of the blue.

Things to Think About

- What do you want your season brochure to say about you?
- What information do you include in your brochure?
- Who gets your brochure? Who could get it that doesn't?

11 Your Newsletter Is Your Best Friend

A nd now we're to the chapter where I create a metaphor and then beat it to death:

An effective newsletter is like a good play.

Okay, so that's really a simile. But you get the idea.

The Plot

Often, when you ask someone to tell you the plot of a story, they'll say, "It was *about* two elderly sisters and their dying hamster . . ." and so on.

People equate plot with "what the play is about"—which differs from theme, which is what the play is *about*. People go to graduate school for years trying to figure out the difference, so let's not even go there. Instead, let's look at plot as a sequence of events—in other words, what's happening. Conveniently, that description makes it a perfect starting point for our metaphor.

The plot of your newsletter would be all the things that are happening with your theatre company: the upcoming show, auditions, administrative notices, board actions, awards, warm-and-fuzzy stuff like marriages, etc. These things make up the content of your newsletter.

People like a good plot that has lots of stuff going on, so try to be diverse and give them lots of different stuff to read about. It's easy to fall into the trap of just promoting your next show. That's an important—if not the most important—reason for publishing a newsletter, but don't let it be the only reason. By giving readers a variety of things to read about, you give them other ways to identify with your theatre. For instance,

- The people you write about begin to take on lives of their own—and that's a major hook. It's the same reason people watch soap operas, sitcoms, or the same nightly newscast over and over again.
- As board actions play out over the long term, readers begin to look for the latest developments.
- Announcements can make readers feel like you care enough about their involvement that you want to keep them updated on things.

Maybe you think your one-and-only task is to sell tickets for the next show. If that's the case, a postcard will do you as much good as a newsletter, and a postcard is cheaper to produce and mail. However, that's a show-to-show approach, even if you've done it for years. A newsletter's advantage over a postcard is that it gets people invested in your theatre and cultivates long-term ticket buyers.

Now, no one likes to watch a play with a boring plot, and no one wants to read a newsletter with boring content. That begins to touch on style, which we'll talk about in a minute, but it also touches on diversity. In other words, what sort of content should you include? Some content I've seen:

- information about the next performance
- comments from the director of the show
- background info on the show itself
- "did you know" fun facts or a quiz about the show
- a spotlight or profile of an actor, techie, volunteer, or donor
- news from the board of directors

- a message from the president or the executive, managing, or artistic director
- a general arts column by one of the theatre's volunteers
- miscellaneous news and notes
- a monthly, quarterly, or annual calendar of theatre events
- a calendar of all local arts events

Some theatres also include advertisements in their newsletters as a way to offset printing and design costs. That's fine, if it works for your company. But one of the nice things about a play is the fact that it's an uninterrupted viewing experience—and some people want the same from newsletters.

Conflict

One thing that makes a play's plot interesting is conflict. Is there conflict in your newsletter? You betcha! But it's probably not the type of conflict you're thinking of. The conflict inherent in your newsletter has real-life stakes for your theatre company, and it boils down to two questions:

- Should your reader read this?
- Should the reader support your theatre?

This sort of conflict is different from the conflict between characters in a play. Nonetheless, conflict between medium and audience is very real.

The second question in particular becomes a high-stakes one if enough people say "no." Hopefully, your newsletter will help them say "yes." In order to do that, though, people must read it.

As a PR person, your job is to create a newsletter that is readable and, ultimately, makes your theatre company as alluring as possible.

Characters

Since I just mentioned characters, let's look at them in the context of our metaphor. The characters in your newsletter are the people you're writing about. They are the cast, crew, musicians, board members, volunteers, and donors who make up your theatre company.

The old rule of characterization applies even to newsletters: Your readers will get to know these people.through what they do, what they say, and what other people say about them. Use all three devices to make your people look good. I can't stress enough how important it is for you to *use your newsletter to play up your people.*

Playing up your people serves two important functions: It gives you the chance to strut your stuff, and it strokes egos. I mean, c'mon, let's face it: most Theatre People have egos (I know that still comes as a shock to some of you). I'm not saying egos are necessarily bad, they're just usually fragile—and this can be a rough business we're engaged in. It never hurts to remind your people they're appreciated. One way to do that is to blow their horns for them.

You can play up your people in a number of different ways, but the common denominator is similar to pitching a news story: Look for the hook. Don't just refer to actors by saying, "The show features Joe Artaud and Diane Ionesco." Play them up. Maybe Joe has won a merit award from the state theatre association, or maybe he's taking to the stage for the first time after serving as a director for ten years. Maybe this is Diane's fiftieth show, or maybe she has returned to the stage after a ten-year retirement. Say something like, "The show pairs veteran actor Joe Artaud with Diane Ionesco, who makes her ACT debut."

If an actor has an extensive performance history with another theatre company in your area—even a competitor—mention it. If an actor is better known in the area as a concert pianist, mention it. If an actor is a founding father or mother of the theatre company, or a board member, or a former board member, or an officer, or a volunteer, mention it.

One of my personal favorites is "award-winning." It's one of the many ways to get lots of mileage out of an award. Even if the actor won the award ten or twenty years ago and has never again attained that level of accomplishment, you can still refer to her as an award winner.

The idea, of course, is success by association. Someone did something cool for *that* show, so they're probably going to do something cool for *this* show: "Hey, this guy won an award for his set designs—I bet he designs some pretty cool stuff. Let's check it out." If I'm doing a Sam Shepard "boot play," and all the costumes are out-of-closet, I'm still going to mention the fact that my costumer won an award for her work on *West Side Story* two years ago (assuming, of course, that she really did).

Success by association also works in another way: If your people are seen as successful, then your theatre looks good for working with successful people.

Over the past three years, I have had the privilege of working with a young lady who has won multiple awards for her choreography, costume design, and performances. She's not even twenty-two and she has built an impressive résumé. You can bet your sweet blisters I work all of that into the newsletter. It usually goes something like this:

> Meredith Van Scoy of Limestone, NY, leads a cast of more than twenty performers.
>
> Van Scoy, a junior English major at St. Bonaventure University, will play The Leading Player, the leader of a troupe of performers who present Pippin's life story.
>
> Van Scoy has appeared in lead roles in BLT's *How I Learned to Bellydance* and *The Fantasticks*. She has choreographed and performed in Bradford's Kiwanis Kapers, and she is a former BCPAC Creative Youth Salute honoree.
>
> Van Scoy will also serve as *Pippin's* choreographer. Earlier this month, the Theatre Association of New York State (TANYS) honored Van Scoy with a Merit Award for her choreography in Wellsville High School's *Oklahoma!* Her choreography in last year's *Cabaret,* produced by Olean Community Theatre (OCT), also earned her a TANYS Merit Award. Van Scoy has also earned TANYS Merit Awards for her acting and costume work.
>
> Later this summer, Van Scoy will work with the Struthers Library Theater in Warren, where she served as a performance intern two summers ago. Last summer, she interned as a technician at the Bristol Valley Theater near Rochester.

That's a lot of stuff to mention, but someone reading the article is bound to recognize Meredith from *somewhere.* I also try to work that material into my press releases without sounding too fluffy (remember: *Fluff bad*).

Another great way to play up your people is through feature stories and profiles. I work with one actor who has more performance notches on his belt than all the rest of the company put together. He built his résumé by getting a lot of fun little cameo roles that didn't involve too much memorization. He doesn't have awards or professional accomplishments to tout, but he's well known in the community and he's one of my very favorite Theatre People. Whenever I write about him, I refer to him as "BLT veteran Dick Marcott." Because he's such a character, he's certainly worthy of attention in our newsletter. Feature stories let you highlight the work of some wonderful people who might otherwise get overlooked.

When you play up your people, you underscore what's probably at least an implied, if not explicit, value of your theatre: You recognize the worth and contributions of your people.

Setting

The setting of your newsletter is the theatre itself. It is the place where things happen. Pretty self-explanatory.

Another aspect of setting is your community. To that end, use the newsletter to play up the local angles of your cast. When appropriate, call attention to people's hometowns. This reinforces the connection between your theatre and the community.

Theme

Theme is "what the play is *about*"—which is different from plot, which is what the play is about (oh, wait, don't get me started on *that* again). A better way to define theme, in the context of drama, would be "what's the play's main idea?" What values does the play espouse, affirm, or call attention to? What's the playwright's vision?

For your newsletter, this relates to your theatre's mission and values. How does the content reinforce, underscore, or affirm your theatre company's values? That sounds hoity-toity, but it's really pretty simple. If your theatre's mission is "to entertain and educate the community," your newsletter needs to call attention to examples of how you're entertaining and educating the community. If your mission is "to provide a creative outlet for community members," your newsletter needs to call attention to examples of how you're providing a creative outlet for community members. In other words, *show your mission in action.*

This requires a good understanding of your mission and a conscious effort to articulate it through the contents of your newsletter. This relates to our next element, dialogue.

Dialogue

Characters talk. It's one of the primary ways of sharing information in a play. But a crucial thing to realize is that it's not just *what* characters say, it's *how* they say it.

The following examples offer variations of the same information, but the way in which the information is said creates different impressions:

> Millersville Players invite you to spend some time enjoying *Dinner with Friends*, the Pulitzer Prize–winning play by Donald Margulies.
>
> The production opens on Friday, March 1, and runs through March 3, with a second weekend of performances beginning March 8.

■ ■ ■

> Millersville Players will present *Dinner with Friends,* the Pulitzer Prize–winning play by Donald Margulies, on Friday, March 1.
>
> "This is a powerful play about two couples who are forced to scrutinize their marriages," says director Jo Jackson. "It's a play for our times."

■ ■ ■

> The first time director Jo Jackson sat down for *Dinner with Friends,* she left her kitchen table feeling a little queasy. "I thought, 'With friends like these, who needs enemies?' ," she chuckles.
>
> But Jackson has spent several months with these friends, and she's inviting you over to join them for an evening at the theatre.

Those are radically different ways of presenting the same basic information. Each has a different feel. Which seems more formal? Which seems more personable? Which seems more engaging? Which grabs your attention? Which gets more hard facts closer to the lead? (Some answers may be used more than once!) You could also mix and match the paragraphs from these examples to create other, different impressions.

Depending on how active Jo is with the theatre and how many times readers have heard about her exploits, people will have very different impressions about the play. If Jo is a well-known "character" to your readers, they may empathize with her more, and her opinion of the show may carry more weight because of the credibility she has with them.

The newsletter is your best form of controlled media for saying what you want about your shows, your people, and your theatre. That's why *a good newsletter is the best form of public relations you can have*. Nowhere can you say what you want to say better and in more depth than in your newsletter. You get to say *what* you want, *how* you want and then give it directly to the people who'll be most receptive.

For that reason, it's crucial to have a good writer write your newsletter. The copy can't just be factual, it needs to be interesting and engaging. It needs to be finessed: conversational style . . . active verbs . . . an appropriate level of sales pitch. It also needs to call attention to as many positive things as possible (but remember: *Fluff bad*): the play's Pulitzers and Tonys and good reviews from the *New York Times;* the positive effect the play has on your company and the community; the unique and positive aspects of the production; the great things your actors and crew have done.

Another important element of newsletter dialogue is *style*. I recommend following Associated Press (AP) style for your newsletter, primarily because then you only need to learn one set of stylistic rules. A couple of other important stylistic rules:

- *Italicize show names.* Show titles should not be in quotation marks, nor should they be underlined or bold.
- *Don't highlight people's names.* I know some folks like to put actors' and techies' names in boldface, but it looks a bit amateurish. If you're playing up your people like you should be, you don't need to bold their names.

At first it may seem as if your newsletter is really just a monologue: you talking to the reader. The reader doesn't have the chance to say anything back. In fact, the reader *does* have the chance to respond. The reader can support your theatre by attending a show, writing a check, or volunteering time. That turns the reader into an active participant in the conversation and, perhaps, even a character within the newsletter itself.

Structure

Structure is how the plot is revealed, the sequence and manner in which the story is told. In your newsletter, that structure equates to the layout.

The most important thing to remember about design is that it needs to be visually appealing. Think back to some of the ideas I mentioned about your "look" in Chapter 9. Your newsletter shouldn't be too busy or cluttered. It should be easy to follow. It should be easy on the eye. It should be attractive.

Most theatregoers today are sophisticated and have a lot of demands on their time. Don't give them a reason to throw away your newsletter. The immediate visual impact your newsletter makes will be the number one reason why they read it or pitch it.

I have seen newsletters that were little more than a big typewritten sheet of legal-size colored paper with news and notes in big paragraphs. They got folded into quarters, slapped on the back with a label, then bundled and dropped in the mail. Yes, that sort of newsletter does get the job done, but is it attractive to look at? Not really. That means fewer people are apt to read it, so it doesn't get its job done as effectively as it could.

The Appendix includes a sample four-page newsletter, plus the front page of a second newsletter. Pay particular attention to some basic design principles:

- *Contrast.* Elements should be juxtaposed for emphasis and to break up the monotony of the page. Contrasting elements shouldn't be just slightly different, they should be radically different so that the contrast seems intentional and not haphazard.
- *Repetition.* Design elements should be repeated throughout the publication to create a sense of sameness and unity.
- *Alignment.* Elements should line up evenly to create strong visual lines that guide the eye. In places where alignment is

broken, it should be for effect and emphasis, not because of random or sloppy placement. Everyone tends to center things, so look for a different way to align your elements.

■ *Proximity.* Things that belong together should be grouped together.

■ *White space.* Beginners tend to think that empty space is a bad thing and needs to be filled. To the contrary, white space helps the eyes rest, provides a way to organize material, directs the movement of the eye across a page, and adds emphasis.

■ *Avoid too many boxes.* A box or two here and there works as a way to call attention to an article, but a page can get *too* boxy. If everything is set apart by its own box, the piece as a whole looks discombobulated and disjointed. One box per page is a good rule.

Spectacle

Let's look at the elements of a play from an Aristotelian point of view (and I'm sure Aristotle would be just thrilled to know I'm using him as an excuse to keep stretching this metaphor). If we do, we can see that a newsletter has spectacle—in other words, bells and whistles. Your newsletter's bells and whistles are its pictures, art, and graphics. Spectacle also includes your color choices. (Aristotle would probably beat me for stretching this metaphor so thin!)

Two-color newsletters are nice, but the most common newsletters I've seen are simple one-color publications, typically printed in black ink. Sometimes they're just the front and back of a piece of paper. Other times, they're four pages, printed on a big sheet of eleven-by-seventeen-inch paper that's folded in half, then in half again for mailing.

The Lake Worth Playhouse in Lake Worth, Florida, has a nice four-page newsletter that's printed in navy blue ink. On white paper, that makes a nice but not overwhelming difference from the typical black. If it were royal blue or some other bright color, it would be too gaudy and hard on the eyes. The color choice serves the theatre effectively.

Another nice but subtle alternative to black is a dark charcoal ink. It's almost black, but it's just different enough to make a publication stand out from others.

One-color newsletters are much more effective if you can offset the text with graphic elements. I like to use poster art on the cover of our newsletter because it gives readers a strong visual element that runs consistently through our PR efforts.

Most theatres don't include photos in their newsletters, but I assure you, it's cheaper than you think, and the benefits outweigh the costs. (We'll talk more about the benefits of pictures in Chapter 14.) Talk to your printer to find out how much it would cost for each photo you add. I particularly recommend using a photo of your president or executive director next to her regular column. That way, people will know what she looks like. It's important to promote your theatre's figurehead this way because it helps personify the theatre. It gives readers a face so they know who they can talk to if they need to see someone in person.

Your logo, as a visual element, is part of the spectacle. In case you skipped Chapter 9, or in case you just plain forgot: Slap that logo on everything! It should be on the cover of the newsletter, in the masthead, on the mailing panel next to the return address, somewhere on the inside, and more.

Music

Since I opened the can of Aristotelian worms, I guess I'd better address music. Except that it just doesn't fit the metaphor. Ya got me on that one.

Next . . . !

Timing

Another aspect of a good play is its timing. Do the elements work together to create a smooth, effective whole? Do the cues happen at the right times? Are the lines delivered at the proper pace? Do the actors mesh in their delivery of lines to each other?

For a newsletter, timing equates to when the newsletter gets mailed. A newsletter that comes out after a show is, obviously, useless as a promotional tool for that show. One that comes out a few days before a show can grab a reader's attention, but the reader may already have plans. Try to get your newsletter into the hands of your readers from ten days to two weeks prior to opening night.

There are two reasons for this: First, a newsletter takes time to read. People must make a conscious effort to sit down and check it out. It may take them a day or three, so give them that time. Second, a newsletter provides lots of information, so readers may need time to digest and think about whether they want to attend, then to check their schedules or find a date. Give them that time.

Newsletters play a key role in a PR campaign. The newsletter gets your audience's attention and lets them know about the show. Your press releases, photos, and advertisements in the newspaper can then serve as secondary sources of information and reminders about the show, reinforcing what they already learned from your newsletter.

Audience

Finally, a good play needs an audience. It's not theatre if it doesn't have an audience. Your newsletter needs an audience, too. By knowing your audience, you can make sure your newsletter gets used to its best effect.

For starters, pay close attention to who's on your mailing list. Why are they there? Do people get your newsletter as a benefit of patronage, or can anyone who asks get it? Do actors and techies get added to the mailing list by virtue of their participation? Who else can you add? You want to make sure folks on the city council get your newsletter—it reinforces your role as an important cultural asset to the community. For the same reason, make sure you send a copy to the chamber of commerce. In fact, give them a bunch so they can distribute copies to people looking for cultural information about the community. You can leave a stack at the library.

Send copies to the arts editor of the local paper, to faculty members at the local college, to English teachers at the high schools, and to presidents of civic groups.

Just make sure you're adding people to your mailing list for a specific purpose, not just because you want a high circulation. Dollar-for-dollar, a newsletter is one of the most effective ways to spend your PR budget, but that's because it's distributed to a targeted, intentionally chosen audience. Your costs can spiral out of control if you don't keep your mailing list culled. Weed out people who've moved away or who haven't attended in a long time. Weed out actors who were added because they were in a show, but who haven't returned in the two years since.

Curtain Call

What is the primary purpose of your newsletter? Is it to promote a show or shows? Is it to keep your patrons updated on the theatre's happenings? Is it a way to cultivate a feeling of belonging among your cast, crew, donors, patrons, and volunteers? It may be a combination of any of these things or something entirely different. Make sure the content and the tone of your writing match the purpose of the newsletter.

Things to Think About

- What purpose does your newsletter serve?
- What type of content does your newsletter have? What could you add that it doesn't already have?
- How does the newsletter's content reinforce your theatre's mission and values?
- Who gets your newsletter, and why are they on the mailing list?
- How is the publication of your newsletter timed to best serve you?

For Further Information

A text I love to use in my media graphics class is Robin Williams' *The Non-Designer's Design Book: Design and Typographic Principles for the Visual Novice,* published by Peachpit Press, 1995. (No, it's not *that* Robin Williams.) The book offers a crash course in basic design principles, using easy to understand and well-illustrated examples. These principles can be applied not only to your newsletter but to all your publications.

12 The Three Ps

The three principal pieces of printing we need to probe in this part of the publication all begin with *p*:

- posters
- postcards
- programs

Are you prepared?

Poster, Poster on the Wall

Posters make a great form of advertising, although they should never be used as the primary form. People tend to overlook them if they're not looking *for* them. If you ask people, "How did you hear about the show," few of them will tell you they saw a poster. But if you ask, "How *else* did you hear about the show" and you give them posters as one of the possible responses, a lot of people will indicate they saw a poster.

Part of the problem is something called "ad clutter." Ad clutter occurs when so many ads get tossed at you that they all blur together so none of them stands out. It happens on TV and in newspapers, and it also happens any place people post fliers and posters. Walk onto any college campus and take a look at a bulletin board—chances are you can't even see the board itself because so many people have posted notices there. Ad clutter can easily swallow your posters.

That means your posters need to stand out. They need to call attention to themselves. They need to be worthwhile.

Posters can vary in size and style, from a one-color photocopy on standard white copy paper to a full-color super-size sheet with brilliant photos and snappy printing. The glitz and glamour of your posters—as well as their size and paper stock—depends on money, sure. But more importantly, before the almighty dollar starts dictating the fate of your posters, you must *make sure your posters reflect your needs*. After all, what's the purpose of a beautiful poster if you don't *need* a beautiful poster?

So, whether you do posters or not, take a moment to consider a few things:

- Why do you use posters—or why don't you?
- Do you have enough posters, or too many?
- Where do you put your posters? Where could you put them?

The best answer to the first question is something like, "They're a cost-efficient and effective way to reinforce our message about the play." In other words, you use posters as part of a larger scheme to get out the word about the show, and it doesn't cost you too much to do it. If you're paying more than a dollar apiece for an eleven-by-seventeen-inch two-color poster, for instance, you're paying too much.

Your posters should reinforce your image. They should have "the look." If everything else you do is glossy and full-color, your posters shouldn't be black-and-white or printed on paper bags. Make every effort to keep your posters consistent with your other printed materials about a show.

If you don't do posters, why not? If it's just a matter of not having a place to put them, read on! If it's a cost issue, scale down the size or scope of the poster, bid the job out to a different printer, or cut back on the number you have printed. If you don't have someone to hang your posters, find someone.

Are you starting to get the idea that I like posters, particularly for smaller theatres? Good, because dollar-for-dollar, posters are a great form of publicity in a small or medium-size town. You can plaster them everywhere without having too many of them printed. We usually have around two hundred posters printed, for instance, and we're hard-pressed to get them all hung.

For bigger theatres in bigger cities, you might need more posters in a larger area, and thus more time to hang them than would be worth your while. That doesn't mean you can't hit places like grocery stores, bookstores, card and gift stores, and other hot spots your audience likes to visit. You can also partner with favorite restaurants in the area. You may find that partnering isn't financially feasible, but I suggest you check it out just in case.

All posters should contain the following information:

- your theatre company's name and logo—right up at the top
- the title of the play and the name of the playwright
- any info you're contractually obligated by the royalty house to include
- times and dates (and days, too, if possible)
- ticket outlets
- ticket prices

I have heard varying ideas about whether to put ticket prices on posters. I used to be opposed to the idea. When people see posters, they typically don't have pens in their hands, which means they're going to have to remember info about the show. Don't force them to remember too much. I don't know about you, but I'm lucky to remember my own birthday, so I'm not going to remember the details about some play I may or may not want to see. If people are going to remember something about the play, I'd rather have them remember the dates than the prices.

But lately I've changed my attitude on the matter. My theatre's ticket prices are one of the best deals in town when it comes to arts and entertainment events. By advertising our ticket prices on our posters, we tell people right up front that they're getting a bargain.

If you have a complex ticket pricing system or reservation information, you may want to include it on the poster, but I encourage you to instead give a phone number or website to contact. You want to use your posters to attract people to the show, not to beat them over the head with minutiae.

It's also wise, if your show has adult subject matter, to include a disclaimer to that effect on the poster.

When it comes time to put up posters, many theatres simply go door-to-door to area businesses, public buildings, and other high-traffic areas and ask to hang their posters. In most instances, this works great. Business owners are usually glad to help. If you're smart, you'll bring along a roll of tape and, if the business will let you, offer to hang the poster yourself. That way, you make sure the poster actually gets up *and* you make sure it gets the best spot available.

But for a variety of reasons, many theatres don't have places around town where they can put posters. If yours is one of those theatres, you can probably resort to phone poles near stop signs (although some towns have ordinances against it) and you can plaster posters over the Post No Bills signs on the walls of vacant buildings . . . but I recommend a different approach: I suggest you conduct a carefully orchestrated campaign to create places to put your posters.

You need to take the same approach you do with fund-raising. Come up with a list of prospective locations, then formally ask about hanging your posters there. Make the "ask" at a time when there's not a show going on, which will free you from any show-related time constraints. Also make sure you bring a sample poster so the business knows what to expect.

Make sure to include all of your business and corporate sponsors on the ask list. If they don't have a public place to hang the poster, see if they'll hang it in the break room, near the water cooler, or in some other place where employees congregate.

Hang posters two to three weeks prior to opening. If you put them up any earlier, the posters will fade into the background of ad clutter that plagues the world today. If you wait any later, people will already have their plans made—and they probably won't include your show.

An important courtesy I should also point out: Make sure someone goes around and takes the posters down after the show closes. Don't assume businesses will take them down themselves, although they often will. But you don't want to be an annoyance, nor do you want to contribute to unnecessary ad clutter, because it damages your future visibility.

Finally, I should mention that posters make great souvenirs for cast and crew members. Some people volunteer to put them up and snatch a couple for themselves while they're at it. I've heard producers and PR people say, "The posters won't do any good if they're hanging in your room. Put them up for the show, then find one you can keep afterwards." But the reality is—and rightly so, I think—people will snag a poster while they can so they don't have to chance it later. Knowing this will happen, all you need to do is make sure you have enough printed so that people who want posters can get them. Yes, it might cost a few extra bucks, but since you're not paying your people, you should at least make sure they get a poster as a memento if they want one.

Postcards from Paradise

Sam Kuba's best friend is the postcard.

When Kuba took over as managing director of Theatre Harrisburg, he faced sagging ticket sales. He and the board members racked their brains for ways to break out of the slump, and they finally decided to resurrect an old idea that had been abandoned several years earlier: sending out postcards before each show.

The first cards, although primitive by Theatre Harrisburg's current standards, produced results. "When these postcards went out, it was like cause and effect. We would have 'this many' ticket sales one day, then the postcards would go out and ticket sales would jump way up here," Kuba says, his hand shooting upward. "So, we decided that's where we were going to put a large percentage of our marketing dollars. We put them out to sixteen thousand households, and they've been extremely successful."

Theatre Harrisburg's postcards have a sophisticated look. "We've now got this down to a fine art of postcards," Kuba chuckles. The postcards, which measure five and a half by eight and a half inches, are full-color and, like any good piece of publicity, they all have a look that's consistent with Theatre Harrisburg's overall image for the season. The front side of each card features an ad for the upcoming show, including artwork, credits, dates and times, sponsorship, and a quick blurb about the show.

"We use the back side for a whole bunch of things," Kuba says. The mailing panel takes up half of the side, and the other half contains notices about other upcoming events, important news about the theatre, or ads for season ticket sales.

"No more than two things on a postcard," Kuba cautions. "I hate to say this, but people don't have the attention span."

Kuba finds that postcards make a great alternative to newsletters. "Newsletters are time and labor intensive," he says. "If I had more time and more money and more staff, we'd do a newsletter. It just wasn't the right thing for us."

Postcards can be used not only as an alternative to newsletters, but also as a supplement. If you do a newsletter for every other show, you might find that it stimulates ticket sales for the first—but then people forget about the second show and ticket sales dip. Use a postcard for the second show as a reminder. Production and mailing costs for a postcard are both lower than for a full newsletter.

Why do a newsletter at all when you could just do postcards? That depends on your company's values. How important is it for your audience and donors to feel connected to the theatre? Postcards make great sales tools, but they don't do much to help people form personal bonds to a theatre company.

If your company opts not to use postcards on a regular basis, you can still use them to great effect as invitations for special occasions. For instance,

- If you're presenting an original play, why not send a postcard to your patrons, subscribers, and donors that includes an invitation from the playwright? Ask the playwright to come up with a list of people she would like to have invitations mailed to, as well.
- If you're presenting a plaque or award to a volunteer, why not send out a postcard recognizing the volunteer and inviting people to attend the presentation? Ask the honoree for names to add to the mailing list.
- If you're doing a dinner theatre production, send out a postcard reminding your subscribers to join you at the restaurant instead of the theatre. You could even let them know the dinner or dessert choices.
- If you're hosting workshops, readings, or presentations by special guests, you can send out postcard reminders to prospective audience members.

■ If you have an annual holiday party for everyone who's participated in your theatre in the past year or two, you can create
holiday-card postcard invitations.

Postcards are also nice because you can leave stacks of them at places
like the library, cafés, and bookstores.

Get with the Program

Programs are to community theatre what beetles are to the insect
world: They come in nine bazillion shapes, sizes, and styles. (Okay,
entomologically speaking, I've exaggerated—there are only some
three hundred thousand beetle species.)

Theatres produce programs as simple as a folded sheet of photocopied paper and as complicated as center-stitched, full-color mini-
Playbills. So what's right for you?

The first thing you need to consider involves an artistic decision:
Are your programs a piece of supplementary, supporting material for
a production or are they an extension of the production?

By an extension of the production, I mean that the program
reflects in mood and image the look of the production itself.
For instance, you could use some neat design ideas in your program for a production of Yasmina Reza's *Art* or Terrence McNally's
Master Class. If you do one of Emily Mann's "Testimony" plays, like
Greensboro, A Requiem, the director and actors could work with you
to create a very personalized and poignant program. Programs for
Nunsense could resemble programs given out by the Little Sisters
of Hoboken. Programs for *The Taming of the Shrew* could look like
they were produced on an old printing press. The possibilities are
endless.

This can get tricky because you don't want to sacrifice your
theatre's look. That overall image needs to transcend any individual
show, and it should take priority in your programs except in the most
extreme of instances.

If your program is a piece of supporting material, removed from
the production, it's much easier to maintain the integrity of your
theatre's look. It's also a much more businesslike, and common, approach to program creation. Nonetheless, as with anything in theatre,

your approach to programs should involve deliberate choice, not happenstance.

The second thing you need to consider is content: What do you put in your program? Why include what you do? Do you sell ads? Why? If you sell ads, do they offset the cost of printing? Do they not only pay for the program but generate extra revenue for the theatre? If you cut back on the content of your program, how much would it reduce printing costs?

The program is one of the first publications you can look to if you need to trim your budget. After all, what do you really need to have in a program? That's a rhetorical question, not a question for you to specifically answer—because I'm sure your list of what you think you need will probably be longer than a list of your actual needs. Here's what really *needs* to be in a program:

- your theatre's name and logo
- the title and author of the show
- a scene breakdown
- a cast list
- intermission information (this is easy to forget, but you should always let folks know if they're not going to have the opportunity for a bathroom break midway through the show)
- production credits for the director, producer, and other individuals who've helped with tech, audience services, and production support
- special thanks
- rules specific to your theatre (no food or drink in the theatre, no flash photography, etc.)
- anything the royalty house contractually obligates you to include

If your program design allows for it, get some artwork on the cover. Use the same artwork you've used for your posters, postcards, website, newsletter, etc. Keep that image consistent.

Chances are you've promised your patrons you'll list their names in the program if they give you money. This is an important schmooze factor, and you should include names if you can, but the reality is that audience members will be able to follow the show with or without the patron list. They might *not* be able to follow if they don't have a scene breakdown, and they're always much more interested in who's playing what role than who gave how much money.

Some theatres print a single list of patrons at the beginning of the season . . . black ink on plain white paper . . . and then insert it into every program during the course of the year. By printing the list all at once, they get a price break on the printing because of the quantity. The inserts also save space within the program itself, which can then be devoted to show-related business.

Other popular items in programs include cast bios (and even photos); information about upcoming events at the theatre; and messages from the show's director, the theatre's artistic director, or the board president. These are all nice things to have—for instance, it's never a bad idea to plug your next show—but they're not always necessary. If you need to cut a corner or two, they could go (and don't let egos get in the way!).

In fact, directors' notes can be problematic. If a show is particularly tricky, you might need some words of explanation or enlightenment from the director. But a director doesn't necessarily have to put a message in the program just because he thinks he can. If you're tight on space, it's better from an institutional standpoint to have a message from one of the bigwigs than from a single director. A message from the artistic director or board president lets you reinforce your theatre's mission and values to the public, so that's not a bad thing, either. As I said, such messages are not crucial, but if you have the space and money, I strongly suggest you include them.

Unless you have lots of space, you might want to think twice about including cast bios. First, Theatre People tend to go on ad nauseam about their own achievements, so you seldom get short bios from them. When you're forced to edit bios, you always end up "butchering" them (just ask the actors). Space certainly isn't a problem when you're doing bios for three actors appearing in David Mamet's *A Life in the Theatre,* but when you do them for the denizens of an entire village for Bertolt Brecht's *The Caucasian Chalk Circle*, you start running into trouble. You don't want to set any precedents with your small-cast shows that you're going to have trouble living with for your large-cast shows.

Finally, if at all possible, I encourage you to list the upcoming events of other arts groups in your area. Why? Choosing to list other events says a lot about your theatre's values—it's a way to put your money where your mouth is when you say you support the arts. Promoting other groups' events promotes a healthier overall arts environment in your area, and that's good for everyone. It's also a good way to attract people who patronize other arts events since arts-minded people tend to support a variety of artistic endeavors.

After you consider content, take a look at design. Make sure your program is easy to follow, that there's a logical progression to the layout. Make sure it's not too cramped, with enough white space to give the reader some breathing room. Big blocks of text are hard to read in a dark theatre, so white space makes it much easier for audience members to quickly consult the program.

Planning Print Jobs

Some final things to keep in mind when you're getting ready to print your posters, postcards, and programs:

- You don't always have to print on white paper. People easily get trapped into thinking they can only use white, but using a colored paper can enhance the artwork. It can be especially effective for designs printed in one or two colors as a way to add an extra color. However, I don't advocate using colored paper just for the sake of it, or even just because it makes posters stand out more—and I certainly warn against using loud, bright, or neon colors. Your paper color should be subtle and have a design purpose.
- Pay attention to the ink color you choose. Black is almost always best, but don't use black just because that's what you're used to.
- Don't go hog-wild with lots of crazy fonts. Just because you have a lot of fonts doesn't mean you should use them.
- White space can be your friend.

After you've evaluated your posters, postcards, and programs (along with your newsletter and brochures) and figured out what you want to do with them, the next step is to visit your friendly neighborhood printer ... conveniently located in Chapter 13.

Things to Think About

- Why do you use posters—or not use them? (And see the rest of the list from earlier in the chapter.)
- Is your ticket information too complex to be easily understood on a poster?
- How can postcards play a role in your overall publicity scheme?
- Do your programs supplement and support a production or are they an extension of the production?
- Do you sell ads for your program? If not, could you?
- Does the program have a message from the artistic director or board president? If so, how does it reinforce your theatre's mission and values?

▙▚ A Few Words About Printing

Make friends with your printer.

I'm not talking computer printer here (although it's never a bad idea to coddle that printer, either). I'm talking about the person who prints your programs and posters and newsletters and all that other fun stuff. Be your printer's friend.

I can't think of anyone who's not directly involved in your theatre company who can potentially cause you more grief than your printer can. Conversely, a good printer can make your company look *really* good. You just cannot overestimate the value of a good printer. I can't stress it enough.

It can be tough to know what to look for in a printer. What makes a good one stand above the rest? What's the best way to work with him? How does all this printing stuff work, anyway?

What to Consider When Choosing a Printer

Customer Service
This will sound like a novel idea to some of you: Price is *not* the single most important factor when choosing a printer. The most important

factor is customer service. That bit of advice should not surprise you coming from someone who's in the customer service business.

I used to oversee a lot of printing—everything from simple business cards and letterhead to a full-color alumni magazine—so I spent a lot of time working with a variety of printers. My reputation depended on the quality of the printed materials I shepherded through production. I wasn't taking any chances; I didn't want to look bad because someone else dropped the ball. So, I worked only with printers who were accommodating and who took care of my needs.

For someone who doesn't do PR for a living, it's even more important to have a printer you can depend on. Your printer has to be someone who will do right by you and your theatre. She has to be someone who doesn't just want your business, but wants your *repeat* business.

A good printer will go through paper samples with you, make last-minute changes or corrections for you without having a hissy fit, do an occasional emergency rush job, and do everything possible to meet the delivery date. These are all invaluable services.

Price

I won't lie. Price is the second most important factor in choosing a printer. Printers can vary wildly in their prices, so you need to shop around. Your best bet is to create a spec (specifications) sheet for a project and send it out for bid. Contact a bunch of different printers and have them give you a price quote.

You can solicit bids one of two ways. You can bid things out project-by-project . . . for instance, a single newsletter edition. Create a spec sheet and find out what each printer will charge you to do that newsletter. Alternatively, you can bid out a package . . . that is, lump a bunch of stuff together and see what kind of deal you can get. Bid out all your newsletters for the year, for instance, or create a list of all your printing needs for the year and see what sort of price you can get. You may get a break on price if the printer knows he will be doing a lot of work for you.

A spec sheet should contain a few simple elements:

- a description of the item to be printed (for example, "four-page newsletter" or "five hundred business cards")
- the number of pages in the item

- the quantity to be printed
- how many colors are to be used (the piece is one-color, two-color, full-color, etc.; include PMS numbers)
- the number of screens to be used (this is when you take one of your colors and you "fade" it so it's a lighter shade than the original color. Screens are used for boxes, lines, and design variations in text)
- whether varnish will be used (varnish is only something you'd do for a full-color publication to help the color "snap," or look sharper)
- the number of photos
- the paper to be used
- the delivery date (when the printer needs to have the product back to you)
- how the publication will be delivered to the printer (on disk? camera-ready copy? Will the printer need to do some layout work?)

Some printers will also label and mail things for you. If you're interested in having that done, include it on the spec sheet for a bid.

A spec sheet lets you compare apples to apples because everyone gives you the same information. You can easily compare the bottom line.

Turnaround Time

Turnaround time is how quickly a printer can return the finished product to you once you give it to him. Here again, printers vary.

If you know when you have to have something ready for distribution, count back two or three days and give that date to the printer. *Always* build in a few days for yourself in case of unforeseen delays. So, if you need something for a Friday night opening, tell the printer you need it on the preceding Wednesday at the very latest; shoot for a week early if you can. This serves double duty: You minimize the chance the publication will be late, and if there's a grievous error that needs fixing, you'll have time to do something about it.

Ask the printer how far in advance you need to get the materials to her. Maybe it's a week; maybe it's two; maybe it's a month. A printer who needs a month needs too much time. A printer who can whip things together in a few days—and do a good job at it—is a godsend (but I don't recommend you test a printer's patience too often by waiting until the last minute).

One thing that will determine turnaround time is the number of proofs you want to see. Figure to add one day to the production process for every round of proofing you go through. The printer sends you the proof, and you look it over and send it back; that's a round of proofing. If there are changes to be made, the printer makes them and sends another proof back to you for review. That's a second round of proofing . . . and typically adds one more day to the production process.

Always see at least one proof. If for no other reason, you want to make sure the printer could read your computer disk okay or that the photos ended up in the right places. Proofs are cheap, and they're good insurance. The printer simply shoots off a laser print for you to look at. If you make changes, get another proof. It's not that you don't trust the printer, it's that you want to make sure the changes were made properly. Believe me, every printer wants your job to be perfect. If there's a mistake, your printer doesn't want it to be her fault, so she isn't going to mind if you take one last look.

For a major publication—such as an annual report or a fund-raising brochure—you might also want to see a blueline. A blueline is a step up from a simple proof, and it's the last thing to happen before the publication goes to press. After a layout is complete, the printer creates plates for use on the press, and for the blueline, he uses a chemical process to create reproductions of those plates. In an ideal world, all proofing is done before you go to blueline because making changes to a blueline costs you money—the printer has to go back and create new plates. But proofing a blueline is still a good idea because it lets you see *everything,* and for something extremely important, it's worth it to have that one last detailed look.

Convenience

Another thing to consider when looking for a printer is convenience. Where is the printer located? Does he deliver? If so, when? Will he pick things up from you? Can you correspond via fax or email? Are the printer's business hours convenient? Yes, the price might be right, but it may be a pain in the patookah to get stuff to the printer. If you're someone who works during the day and can't get to the printer during his normal business hours, then working with that printer will turn into a chore.

Politics

Alas, the evil "P" word. But politics is a reality you need to consider. Folks in your community, particularly if it's a small town, expect you to do business in your community. It's that "all for one, one for all" mentality.

The problem, of course, is that the local printer might be waaay more expensive than one in the next town over. Or he might do a crappy job. Or she might be a pain in the neck.

If you sell ads in your program, a printer might buy a big ad from you. You can't very well turn around and have the program printed somewhere else, can you? Or worse yet, a printer underwrites the cost of your program in exchange for an ad, then does a sloppy job.

I've also known situations where someone on the board of directors works for a printer and tries to throw business in that direction. Gosh, if you don't do business with that printer, aren't you in essence affecting the board member's livelihood? Sometimes people need to be reminded to keep the theatre's interests separate from their own.

Sometimes, for political reasons, you may have one printer do some of your work, like your newsletters, and another printer do other things, such as programs. There's nothing wrong with sharing the wealth a little bit, but don't spread yourself too thin.

Whatever you do, don't let politics trap you into using a bad printer. We're talking about your theatre's image here, and that's one of the most important assets your theatre has. Don't piddle it away through bad printing.

What to Look for in Print Jobs

The other consideration you need to keep in mind when choosing a printer is the quality of the craftsmanship. When evaluating a printer's work, pay particular attention to how well the photos and graphics reproduce, how close the color matches your specs, how well the color registration matches up, and how well the piece is assembled.

Photos and Graphics

Photos should be clear, and neither too light nor too dark. If they're in color, the reproductions should match the original photos (they may appear too yellow, too cyan, or too magenta, which affects overall color quality).

Pictures should also be right-side up and they should not be flipped—printed as a mirror image. I've seen instances where some-one facing left, for instance, ended up facing right because the picture got flipped.

Graphics should be clear, with no bit-mapping or computer pix-elization. The edges should be smooth and not choppy.

Color

All colors should match your PMS specification. Color coverage should be uniform. It shouldn't have streaks or fading (such as when a laser printer or photocopier runs out of ink, and some of the page prints out fine while other parts are faded).

The ink should not be smudged. Smudging usually means a publication was assembled before the ink dried.

If you used more than one color, do the colors line up? This is called registration. A poorly registered publication looks like cheap 3-D gone wrong.

Assembly

Pages should be trimmed neatly. Nothing should be chopped off. Folds should be crisp, even, and not crooked. Edges and corners should not be mangled.

Staples should be firmly fastened and positioned in the proper places. If the publication is perfect-bound rather than stapled, there should be no glue oozing out of the binding.

Final Tips

Once you've chosen a printer, whether for a single job or a season's worth of stuff, visit the print shop in person. Ask for a tour. This serves two important functions:

- Going behind the scenes helps you learn about the printing process. If you can demystify the process and get an under-standing of what's involved, you'll have more realistic expec-tations about what your printer can do for you.
- Going into the printer's world will give you some insight into the printer herself. It's a way to get more comfortable with her and build a working relationship.

If all goes well and you're happy with the printer's work, you should be able to build a successful relationship with the printer that will lead to a kind of shorthand between the two of you. That makes the production process *so* much easier. The printer will also be willing to go the extra mile for you, which can be a real bonus when you find yourself in a printing pinch.

Another good tip: never order huge amounts of stationery, envelopes, etc. If you change your logo, phone number, or Web address, you'll be stuck with a bunch of printed materials that have outdated information. There are ways around such a conundrum, but it's better if you don't put yourself in that position. Order enough materials to get you through six months, but never order more than a year's supply.

Finally, if you value the work your printer does for you, let him know. A thank-you card never hurts. A mention in the "special thanks" section of your program doesn't hurt, either. Let your printer know—just as you would with a volunteer, a donor, or a stagehand—that his good work makes a difference.

Things to Think About

- What materials does your theatre company have printed? Include everything: letterhead and envelopes, business cards, brochures, posters, fliers, newsletters, etc.
- Why do you use the printer you use?
- How happy are you with your printer's customer service?

14. Picture This

I suppose I could've put photographs in Chapter 12 and called it "The Four Ps," but the "ph" sound just didn't seem to fit. Darn those phonics.

But it's not just because of the "ph" sound that photographs didn't fit. The three Ps deal with publications, and your photographs should be used for a whole lot more.

A Picture is Worth 2,623 Words

Let me start by getting the cliché out of the way: A picture is worth a thousand words (or, at least in this chapter, photography is worth 2,623 words). Photos show people things about your production that words alone cannot. They show sets and costumes. They show action. They show familiar faces. As a design element, photos serve several important functions. They break up the page. They call attention to stories.

You can use three kinds of photos:

- a candid or action shot (a photo of something as it's happening)
- a posed shot (a photo you set up)

- a mug shot (a person's close-up, typically a head-and-shoulders shot)

You shouldn't have a problem getting the hang of candid or posed shots, although I recommend that a professional photographer take any mug shots you need since mug shots tend to be used for official or high-profile purposes. Make sure your board members all have their mug shots taken. For theatres with a paid staff, key staffers should also have their mug shots taken. Should you ever need mug shots for publicity purposes, it's good to have them on hand ahead of time so you can respond quicker.

You'll have plenty of opportunities to use photos in your PR efforts: in your newsletter, on your website, in displays, and to accompany news releases. We'll talk about those various functions in a minute. But first, before we can use photos, we need to take them.

Camera One

You don't need to shoot pictures for *Life* magazine to do competent photography for your theatre. You don't even need fancy equipment. I suggest your theatre invest in a midrange point-and-shoot camera with an interchangeable zoom lens, which you can get at a discount store for about $250. I suggest an interchangeable lens because it will make your life easier down the road. As you get better at photography, you may decide that a more powerful zoom lens will help you snag better pictures. Spend the extra bucks and get a camera case, too.

Cameras in the thirty-dollar to fifty-dollar range—or worse yet, disposable cameras—aren't going to do the job for you. They don't have lenses that will let you zoom, crop, and tweak the way you need to.

I do not recommend a digital camera, even though they're all the rage. If you were putting photos only on the Web, then maybe. But you'll need hard copies of most of your photos, which means you'd need to have a super high-quality printer to go with that digital camera. Don't sacrifice your photo quality just for the sake of technology.

Picture Perfect

Once you start snapping pictures, you'll see how simple it is. Just keep in mind a few easy-to-remember tips:

- *Get closer.* Most people tend to take pictures from too far away. That makes the subjects smaller than they need to be. If you get closer, we can see faces better.
- *Zoom in.* When most people take pictures, they capture a lot of extra space around their subjects. Who cares about the room or the background . . . the focus should be on the people in the picture.
- *Proximity.* Space gets easily exaggerated in a photo, so two people standing five feet apart look like they're standing on opposite shores of the Atlantic. Get people to move toward each other; it may feel too close in person, but the photo will look much better. Eliminating vacant (and wasted) space focuses the viewer's attention.
- *Angles.* Angles make people and things more interesting to look at.
- *Levels.* We're all used to looking at the world from a height of five to six feet, give or take a few inches. If you climb up on something high and shoot down, or if you lie on the ground and shoot up, you can capture some nifty perspectives.
- *Action.* Pictures of people standing around look boring. Particularly dreadful are group shots where everyone clumps together and smiles at the camera. Capture action because that captures people's attention.
- *Background.* What's happening in the background? Is there something that's distracting or inappropriate? Does it look like a tree branch is sticking out of the side of someone's head? Often we're so busy looking at the subject that we forget to take a quick look at what's going on behind her.
- *Tidiness.* Do a quick check: Are the buttons all buttoned? Is his fly zipped? Is her hair brushed? Is anyone's underwear showing by accident? These little things can ruin an otherwise perfect picture.
- *Light.* Is it bright enough? Most good cameras will let you know if you need the autoflash. Sunlight offers great hues, so if you can take pictures outdoors, great. Cloudy days are best because

clouds diffuse the light better. Morning and late afternoon light creates interesting shadows. Indoors, avoid fluorescent light if possible—it makes photos come out with a greenish tint. Colored stage lights can also be tricky.

Consider the purpose of the photos to decide whether to shoot in color or black-and-white. If they're just for the Web, shoot in color. If they're for submission to the local newspaper or for use in your newsletter, shoot in black-and-white because the photos will reproduce better.

Black-and-white can be tougher and take longer to get developed than color, so scope out a developer well ahead of time. Find out how long the turnaround time for developing will be and take that into account when you're planning publicity.

"Whether the images are in black-and-white or color, your subjects should wear mid tones to deeper colors so their faces are the prominent showpiece," advises Glenn Melvin, executive director of the Professional Photographers Society of New York State. "If they're wearing costumes, again the face is still the main thing to accentuate. If colors are in the costume, try to get a color in the background that brings out that color in the clothing being worn. But always remember, people looking at pictures like to see faces."

The Appendix offers several samples of good and bad photos. By following the examples, you can start taking better pictures right away.

I also discovered that the more photos I took, the better I got. It's like anything, I suppose—practice improves performance. Another secret I learned is to take a lot of pictures. Take more than you think you need. If you take a slew of photos, *something* is bound to turn out okay.

Picture This

So you know how to take better photos. Now, what do you take pictures of?

- For starters, you can take photos during rehearsals, then use them to create sandwich-board or bulletin-board displays in local libraries, supermarkets, bookstores, etc.—even in the lobby of your theatre. It's a great way to generate buzz about the show.

- As it gets closer to dress rehearsal, take photos of a few of the actors in costume, then submit them to the local paper to advance the show.
- If you have ornate costumes or a beautiful set, take archival photos of those things. Definitely take those pictures in color.
- Get everyone on stage in costume and take a big cast photo. From an aesthetic point of view, cast photos are usually pretty gruesome, but they make great mementos for people working on the show. You can even sell copies to cover the cost of the photographs.
- Take photos at special events. Get pictures of the theatre board's officers schmoozing with donors.
- If a company or board member gets a special award, take a picture. Do an action shot of the actual award presentation, then stage a photo or two to have just in case.
- You just bought new lighting instruments? Get a photo of someone installing or testing them.

Don't be afraid to use that camera. Take pictures whenever you can.

Schmooze on Film

Another important function photos can serve for you is their schmooze value. People feel important when they have their pictures taken. If someone makes a major donation to the theatre, stage a simple check presentation using a fake check or an envelope—people looking at the picture will never know the difference, and the scene is intended only to be symbolic of the actual check presentation, anyway.

What do you do with a photo like this? Newsletter. Website. If it's a *really* major donation, send it to the local newspaper, although I'll warn you again that most papers *hate* photos of check presentations. If you want a photo to send out with a press release, take a picture of the donor doing something in the theatre, maybe trying on costumes or inspecting the light board. If the donor has earmarked the gift for something, take a picture that relates to the gift's purpose.

Donors love to have their photos taken—or maybe they just figure it's part of the gig. Whatever the case, don't pass up the chance to cultivate goodwill by using your camera.

A schmooze photo doesn't have to be of a donor, either. It could be of a special guest, a favorite volunteer, or the visiting governor who just happened to be passing through. Schmooze on film!

Working with the Pros

If you hire a professional photographer to come in for a particular purpose, there are a few things you can do to facilitate the experience. After all, most photogs work on the clock, although some charge by the job. Try to make the shoot smooth for everyone.

"Photographing for PR is usually a last-minute thing. This actually should be one of the first things done so you can get started with your PR," says Glenn Melvin. "Usually costumes are either being made or don't come in until close to the play date. If the photography could be done early in the rehearsal process, the photographer won't be rushed to get images ready for the play."

Sometimes, as in mug shots, subjects won't be wearing costumes at all. "If you are unsure about what to wear for the session, either bring many items or have a consultation prior to the session," Melvin suggests.

Don't assume the photographer knows what to shoot. "If the photographer hasn't seen the play, some explanation will help so the photographer knows what type of character this is and what kind of facial expressions to look for," Melvin says. "The interaction of the characters is important and could be scripted for the photographs."

And, Melvin adds, you don't necessarily have to settle for what you see: "With the advent of digital photography and computers, not only can we take photographs, we can also add any artwork, a title, or actor's name to the images. We can also adjust color and contrast."

Some photographers will be willing to work out an exchange for their services, perhaps a logo in the program or a display in the theatre's lobby. They may be able to recoup the cost of time and supplies by selling copies of the photos they take to cast and crew members. If nothing else, you can probably get a nonprofit rate. Talk to your photographer and see what ideas he's open to.

I Have These Pictures—Now What Do I Do with Them?

You have all sorts of places to use your photos, even if you don't yet realize it.

Newsletters

Photos spice up a newsletter and make it look much more professional—as long as the newsletter is printed, not photocopied.

A photo can do a nice job of drawing attention to a special event or person. If you do a feature story on a volunteer, include a photo of the person, preferably an action shot rather than a mug shot. If the theatre has an annual holiday gala, include a picture of it. There's probably not a whole lot you can say about an event like that, but a photo can be a nice way of giving it some extra attention. If your company goes off to perform at a state or regional festival, take pictures. Print them in the newsletter so folks can share the fun and excitement.

Do you give away any scholarships? Take a photo of the recipient talking with someone from your board or staff. If you can't make that happen, try to at least get a mug shot of the recipient that you can use along with a story.

Do you have a message from the board president or artistic director in the newsletter? Then include a mug shot, too. Your president or artistic director needs to be a recognized and high-profile figurehead. Including a photo encourages recognition.

If you get new equipment, print a photo that shows the equipment in use or being installed. Let people know about the improvements you're making to the theatre by *showing* the improvements. If donations made the purchase possible, that's all the more reason to print a photo–*show* the donors you're being a good steward of their money.

Website

Your website gives you a chance to use color photos to make the theatre look snappy and fun. The Web is a highly visual medium, so the more photos—and the greater the variety of photos—you can include on your site, the better. Just don't use so many photos that the site looks crowded or busy, or takes too long to load.

Anything you include in your newsletter should also find a place on the website: text *and* pictures. The Web is also a great place to archive photos so that former actors and crew can log on and revisit their former glory. While they're at your website, something else—like an audition date or a subscription opportunity—might catch their eye.

Brochures

If you have a stockpile of photos, you may find use for them in your brochure. You can use color or black-and-white, although the design of the brochure may lend itself to one over the other.

Newspapers

When you're sending out a press release about a show, it's nice to include a black-and-white photo or two. The newspaper may want to send its own photographer, but if it can't, you can offer a Plan B by providing your own photos.

Make sure the photos show interesting action. Who cares if Joe Smith is the lead—is he doing anything interesting and photogenic? The paper would much rather have a picture of Mary Brown eating fire or of Sam Wilson and Pat O'Shea swinging from the scaffolding.

Displays

Most serious actors have a glamour shot (a mug shot that makes them look like An Actor). It's nice to do a display in the theatre lobby that includes glamour shots so audience members can see the actors out of costume and without makeup. Remember, this is *community* theatre, and folks in the community like to see who else from the community is in the show.

If the cast is large, you might only display glamour shots of the leads. If the people in your company don't all have glamour shots, arrange to have glamour shots taken. Call in a local photographer to do them for you, since these photos really should be spiffy and professional. If actors want to buy their glamour shots once the show is over, photographers are usually happy to oblige.

End of the Roll

If you're like me, you never have enough time for anything—but it's a worthwhile investment to take the time to take better photos. Just carry the camera around with you for a while and shoot whatever strikes your fancy. It doesn't even have to be at the theatre—just shoot, shoot, shoot.

As time passes, your theatre will develop a photo archive. Come up with a way to keep the archive organized so you can find photos easily. Hunting for a photo that's six or seven years old can be a time-waster: "I just *know* it's here *some*where!" If people want to borrow photos from the archive, have them sign them out. You can even go so far as to make photocopies of the borrowed photos and have the borrower sign off on the copies. Then you'll know exactly who has which photos.

Theatre is basically a visual medium, so it only stands to reason that photos can help you promote your theatre. Look for ways to offer photos that are as interesting and exciting as the theatre you present.

Things to Think About

- What kind of camera can your theatre afford?
- Looking at the list of photo tips, where do you need to improve the most?
- What special events does your theatre sponsor that you could photograph?
- How can you use photographs to cultivate positive feelings among donors? Among volunteers? Among cast and crew?
- How can photos improve your publications?
- What sort of organizing system can you develop for your photos?

◢▟◣ Bright Ideas

I have been fortunate to have literally hundreds of community theatres share their PR and marketing success stories with me, and I'd like to pass along to you some of the most interesting ideas from the bunch. (In other words, I want to sit back for a few pages and let other people do some of the work.) My intent is to spark some creative out-of-the-box thinking on your part. Don't just look at these ideas as examples, look at them as things you can adapt to your own shows, seasons, and situations.

And so, without further ado . . .

Etc., Etc. . . .

Think about the last conference or convention you attended (even something like a home-and-garden show or a sportsmen's show). If you're like most people, you went around the exhibition hall and collected goodies from the various exhibitors and vendors. Who knows what you might ever do with all those pins, buttons, and pens . . . but it's hard to resist picking up one of everything.

That's because people like to get stuff. Use that to your benefit. If you can afford it, have some sort of little freebies created with your name on them. Then, give them away

- to your donors and subscribers as a special bonus for their support
- to audience members who come to a particular show
- as party favors at your annual meeting
- as a way to commemorate a special anniversary season
- at arts galas
- when you do an appearance for a local service organization

Where do you get freebie stuff made? You may have a local vendor, or you can check out one of many catalogs. Or, of course, you can look on-line (just type in something like "pencils" in a search engine and see what you get!). Look for things you can print the theatre's name on and, if possible, its logo. On some items, you might even be able to fit the Web address.

Popular freebies include

- bumper stickers
- can coolies
- combs
- key chains
- pens and pencils
- plastic cups
- rulers
- sticky notes

If you want to get more elaborate, you might consider

- Frisbees
- golf balls
- license plate holders
- mouse pads
- stress balls

You can even have chocolates made with special wrappers.

■ ■ ■

Refrigerator magnets make great giveaways. They get hung in highly visible places, and they're a handy way for people to keep track of their tickets: Just hang 'em on the fridge with the magnet.

A few years ago, Olean Community Theatre (OCT) in Olean, New York, had nice magnets made. About the size of a business card and oriented horizontally, the magnets have OCT's logo, mailing address, and phone number (if they were made today, I would suggest adding the Web address, too). According to OCT president Fior Zinzi, the magnets were a hit. "We sent them in with season tickets to our subscribers," she explains. "We did it for two years. It worked well for us."

The Wilmington Drama League (WDL) in Wilmington, Deleware, had magnets made up for its sixty-fifth anniversary. A friend of the theatre who was working for a large credit card company was able to persuade one of the company's suppliers to do the magnets as a donation. The same size as OCT's but oriented vertically, the magnets had WDL's logo, contact info, and sixty-fifth anniversary logo (developed free by a local PR firm). The magnets also included the slogan "Community Theatre: You Make It Happen."

"Like so many community theatres out there, we wanted to attract a younger audience," says Ted Wilson, managing director for WDL. "We figured younger audience members would also have families and children. With all that 'refrigerator art' out there, what could be better than yet another refrigerator magnet? We also thought it would work with our traditional, more senior audience members, too, because they have grandchildren."

An alternative are calendar magnets with your name and logo at the top. Some companies also offer novelty magnets of different sorts. Check 'em out on-line.

■ ■ ■

If a calendar magnet isn't your thing, what about a regular calendar? Vendors offer personalized calendars in a number of styles. With any calendar, it's natural to have show dates and auditions dates conveniently printed right on them.

Many vendors offer wall calendars. Most come with stock photos (like wild animals or nature scenes), and your theatre gets its name and contact info printed on each page. Other vendors offer more elaborate packages, including the option to add your own photos (but that gets expensive).

I've also seen day-by-day desk calendars that have the theatre company's name and logo at the top of each page, along with a quote of the day. Special holidays are appropriately labeled, and the calendar printer will also add events and highlights as you request, so you can get the theatre's season dates on there. These make nice gifts.

Another alternative are pocket-sized datebooks. I know a lot of salespeople in the radio biz who give datebooks away to their preferred clients.

■ ■ ■

One of my favorite gift items are lapel pins, which come in several styles and are much cheaper than you'd suspect. You can have the theatre's name or logo cast into or engraved on a pin. They come in gold or silver hues, and some styles even include color. Pins are *very* classy and cool.

Think of the types of groups that have lapel pins: Rotary Club, Kiwanis Club, Lions Club, fraternities and sororities, etc. It's a special symbol of membership, so people feel like real theatre insiders when they get a pin from *their* theatre.

■ ■ ■

As long as we're mentioning civic organizations, let's not forget that they're always looking for ways to interest and entertain their members at meetings. Senior citizen centers and nursing homes are also always on the lookout for entertainment.

Call your local civic clubs and ask to do a quick performance at one of their lunch meetings. It need only be a five- to ten-minute excerpt from a play or one or two songs.

There are also special interest clubs, like the Current Events Club, the Women's Literary Club, or the local Hoo-Ha Club, that might be interested in having someone from your theatre as their guest. Some theatres even go to local city council meetings or chamber of commerce meetings to do short performances.

Don't forget to take tickets with you. You'll have a captive and enthusiastic audience. (But even if you don't sell many tickets, you usually get a free meal out of the deal!)

■ ■ ■

Many bookstores host performers, whether it be the next Bob Dylan and his acoustic guitar or poets reading their own work. Take advantage of any opportunities your local bookstores offer. People who go to bookstores tend to have extra spending money, be better educated, and be more likely to patronize an arts event (sounds like "knowing your audience," doesn't it?). Even if the store hosts only musicians, maybe it's just because no actors have ever asked.

Bookstores can also serve as a great place for displays. I was recently in Buffalo, where one of the Barnes and Noble stores had a neat *Romeo and Juliet* display that tied in with a production being done by a local theatre. The bookstore got to strut its stuff and show off the Shakespeare-related resources it had, and the theatre got a nice plug.

■ ■ ■

How about bookmarks? Have them printed with your season's shows and dates and a contact number for ticket information. Put your Web address on there, too.

Ask local bookstores to be distributors. Ask the local library to give bookmarks away to all its patrons for two weeks . . . or even a month. If there's a college in town, ask its library to participate, too.

"We put some in local libraries, left them out on a display table along with our scrapbooks at our productions, took them to theatre conferences, and left some on the counter of our local Muncie Civic Theatre [MCT], a seventy-year-old community theatre here," says Judy Schroeder, artistic director of the Heartland Stage Company in Muncie, Indiana.

Schroeder says MCT got in on the act, too. "MCT had some lightweight bookmarks printed for its season as a run-off on the edge of the paper left over after printing their season brochure. They just asked the printers if they would do it, and the printer did it for free! They were on lightweight, glossy paper with four or five colors. The moral: 'Never pay for advertising until you ask if someone will do it for free.'"

Make sure you print enough bookmarks so that no one runs out after a day or two.

If you want to get really fancy, you can give away leather bookmarks with foil printing. I've also seen brass bookmarks. These, obviously, aren't cheap to give away, but they make beautiful gifts for donors and subscribers. Instead of having the season printed on leather or brass bookmarks, as you would with paper bookmarks, put the theatre's name and logo on them. Keep them simple and formal.

■ ■ ■

People like to get things. They also like to *win* things.

ACTORS, Inc., in Ames, Iowa, raffles off a night on the town. For each show, one lucky season subscriber wins dinner for two, a chauffeur-driven limo, and flowers. Alton Little Theater in Alton, Illinois, raffles off cruises. The Little Theatre of Mechanicsburg sold fifty-dollar raffle tickets for a trip to New York City and a weekend's worth of Broadway shows.

Such raffles are a way to get your theatre's name out to people who might not otherwise be interested in seeing your shows. After all, someone may not care much about your production of *Kiss Me, Kate!,* but she might find the possibility of winning a cruise alluring. At worst, her raffle purchase gives your theatre a couple of extra bucks; at best, you've found a new lifetime supporter of the theatre.

■ ■ ■

How about starting the morning with a fresh cup o'Joe, sipped from a nifty ceramic mug with your theatre's name on it? That's how supporters of the Theatre of Dare in Nag's Head, North Carolina, start their day. (If you're like me, you quaff Diet Mountain Dew from your mug late into the night while writing book chapters.)

"We found a deal through a local promotions company. We thought they would last for several years, but we actually sold better than half of them the first year," says theatre president Kathy Morrison. "Admittedly, most of the sales were to active members, a few sold from the lobby during the shows, and we sold some to family members."

The mugs are white, adorned with the theatre's name and logo in green, and glazed over with a protective shell. "They only cost us about a dollar-fifty each, including shipping—it was a deal—and we can sell them for four dollars," Morrison says. "The 'official' Theatre of Dare mug has become a great way for our folks to 'show the colors.'"

This year, the theatre has something new in store for the mugs. "We're going to give them as a thank-you gift for our second level of donations and up and have people pick them up at a sponsor's table during the first performance. That may well cause other sales as well," Morrison says.

■ ■ ■

The Fulton Opera House in Lancaster, Pennsylvania, offers Cat's Meow Village replicas of the theatre. Each wooden replica depicts the façade of the opera house and is cut out to match the building's outline. People collect Cat's Meow cut-outs like crazy, and collectors typically tend to have at least some disposable income (which makes them more likely to be theatregoers).

A couple of counties away, the Little Theatre of Mechanicsburg also has wooden cut-outs, with artwork based on a rendering by local artist Clarence Rebenstorff (the original rendering hangs in the theatre lobby). Local artisan Jeannie Dorsey does the cut-outs, which come in two sizes: regular for fifteen dollars and large for twenty.

■ ■ ■

Speaking of renderings, the Pier One Theatre in Homer, Alaska, had a beautiful painting of its theatre done by artist Brad Hughes for its twentieth season in 1993. The painting hangs in the theatre's lobby, but Pier One offers prints for sale. "We also give posters to individuals, contributors, businesses, etc., as a recognition of their partnership with us," explains artistic director Lance Petersen. "We're using the image on a postcard/rack stuffer, and on the other side, we're printing the season schedule or, if left blank, a handwritten message for response to inquiries, donations, applications for youth theatre, and many other uses."

The image also adorns Pier One's website <*www.xyz.net/ ~lance*>. At first it appears on screen as a black-and-white sketch, but as the page continues to load, a full-color version appears.

■ ■ ■

A number of theatre companies produce T-shirts, or sweatshirts, or polo-style shirts to commemorate their shows or seasons. Shirts make neat advertising before a show, and they turn into popular souvenirs afterwards. I have one friend with Olean Community Theatre (OCT) who has a decade's worth of shirts. Whenever he's involved with a new show, he wears all his past shirts like badges of honor.

Shirts may have just the theatre's name and the title of the production. OCT's shirts feature poster art screen-printed on the front (the art includes the theatre's name and logo).

At community theatre festivals, I've seen special shirts that companies had made up to commemorate the event. At one state festival, members of Albany Civic Theatre from Albany, New York, had baseball caps for their production.

Some companies make shirts for cast, crew, and theatre members only; others sell leftovers in the lobby during the run of the show.

■ ■ ■

"Our main source of PR tends to be placemats, which we print up and deliver to restaurants to use for free," says Steve Helsel, operations manager for Altoona Community Theatre in Pennsylvania. "We average about twenty thousand placemats per show, which we deliver about two weeks prior to show weekend, just before the box office is ready to open."

"We stopped using posters for a while because they can be a pain to distribute," Helsel adds. "We have recently started using the placemat design, however, and getting a certain number of them printed as posters on a better stock of paper. The number varies according to how many we think we have the time to deliver, the cast size, and whether the cast can help."

■ ■ ■

Take a regular sheet of copy paper. Cut it in half (either direction works). Now take one of the half sheets of paper and fold it in half along the shorter axis. Ta-da! You have a table tent. You can fold over a small strip along the bottom edge of each side and tape those edges together if you want greater stability. Once you get the basic idea, don't be afraid to experiment with sizes. You can also create a table tent by taking a sheet of copy paper, folding it into thirds, and taping the two edges together.

Put artwork on each panel of your table tent. Include your name and logo in a prominent spot, and don't forget dates, times, and ticket info. Then, put your table tents on every table in every restaurant that will give you permission.

■ ■ ■

The Spirit of Broadway Theatre in Norwich, Connecticut, gets its sponsors to help promote shows.

The theatre creates "sponsor flyers," which measure 3.5 inches by 11 inches; three of them fit horizontally on a sheet of standard copy paper. The fliers have the show's title and artwork, the theatre's name and logo, show dates and times, ticket prices, and contact info. Each sponsor gets a stack of these fliers, which they distribute to their customers via shopping bags, bank envelopes, etc.

■ ■ ■

"Sandwich board, baby!"

That's the word from Tony Allegretti, marketing director for Theatre Jacksonville in Florida. Allegretti's sandwich board, which measures two feet by four feet, sits atop a circular brick dais on the street corner next to the theatre. The sandwich board features the name of the current show in big, bold letters. "Our location is prime," Allegretti says. "Sixty thousand people drive by in a week. You can't beat it."

Bradford Little Theatre in Pennsylvania uses sandwich boards at its ticket outlets, the city library, and the biggest supermarket in town. The boards have BLT's name and logo painted at the top, then they staple posters, ticket information, and candid photos taken during rehearsals into the corkboard. They try to capture as many people on film as possible so that as many faces as possible appear on the sandwich boards. A passerby is bound to recognize *someone* in the pictures. On the boards placed at ticket outlets, BLT also includes a sign that says, "Tickets on sale here!"

■ ■ ■

The Fulton Opera House in Lancaster, Pennsylvania, promotes its shows by getting into party mode. Local hosts, typically season ticket subscribers or board members, host a dinner party with the actors. "It's the idea of you inviting your circle of friends," says Rod McCullough, the Fulton's managing director. "It's usually a thirty-to fifty-people thing."

The actors sing or perform for the dinner guests. "It's a real sneak preview, only for them, and they get really excited about it," says Patricia Fackler, the Fulton's director of marketing and PR.

The parties vary depending on the show, and sometimes they're held in a location like an old church rather than in someone's home.

"For *The Sound of Music* we did a family thing," says Fackler. "Someone who was very kid-oriented hosted it and invited a dozen families to their home."

The host underwrites the entire event, Fackler explains. "It's very generous on their part," she says. "But they also get to show off for their friends a little, too. They do it as a service to the theatre and to be able to have a unique party—because people do talk about it for weeks. And these are typically people who do entertain anyway, so it's not that difficult to pull off. We try not to make it a difficult process."

"And they can choose the level of poshness," McCullough adds. Events have varied from just hors d'oeuvres to full dinners to picnics for kids.

"And the one thing it does not do is take up a lot of staff time," Fackler adds with a laugh. "I do a little coordination, but other than that, that's it. That's really important for us."

■ ■ ■

Don't forget that your public service or education mission can serve as a way to get extra publicity.

The Reading Community Players in Reading, Pennsylvania, see their mission as a chance to stimulate public discussion about important topics. "We've been having public speakers before some of our shows to have an open discussion about the show topics," says Denise Smaglinski, RCP's business manager. "Before *I'm Not Rappaport* we had someone from the Office of Aging; before *The Boys Next Door* we had a mildly retarded man who has lived in supervised residences; before *Angels in America*, Berks AIDS Network sent a different speaker prior to each performance. Audiences have been very receptive to the speakers."

When RCP gave a production of *A Lesson Before Dying* at the Reading Area Community College campus, the college sponsored a panel discussion on capital punishment. "On the panel were our director, an actor, and several well-known and outspoken members of the community" says Smaglinski. "It was fairly well attended and was covered on a local news station."

But that wasn't all. "This same show was performed gratis at our county prison for the inmates and staff there. It certainly wasn't helpful in drawing a new audience, but it was an amazing venue, my favorite to date."

■ ■ ■

While some shows lend themselves to serious (and important) public discussion, others lend themselves to fun gimmicks. For instance, if you're doing *The Pajama Game,* give an admission discount to audience members who come to the show in their pajamas (but beware the folks who sleep in the buff!). If you're doing *Little Shop of Horrors,* give a discount to people who bring flowers to the show, which you can then turn around and deliver to a local hospital or nursing home. I've heard of a *Bye Bye Birdie* golf open, a blood drive for *Dracula,* and targeted marketing to accounting and tax firms for *Love, Sex and the IRS.*

The Tacoma Musical Playhouse in Tacoma, Washington, offers "Lunch with the Cast." People can have lunch with the likes of Little Orphan Annie, Professor Harold Hill, and other main characters.

When the Billings Studio Theatre in Billings, Montana, did *The Wizard of Oz,* it held dog auditions for the role of Toto. Byron Civic Theatre (BCT) in Byron, Illinois, did the same thing; for *Annie,* a BCT board member shaved Daddy Warbucks' head on stage. When BCT did *Cinderella,* it held a children's tea with the title character.

The Corn Stock Theatre in Peoria, Illinois, incorporates "surround entertainment" as part of its shows. "Corn Stock Theatre is located on public parkland," explains theatre manager Cindy Hoey. "It is an outdoor theatre but protected from the elements by a large circuslike tent. This year we decided to try to make the environment as entertaining as the show itself."

So for *Damn Yankees,* a local organization called the Old-Timers' Baseball Association came out to usher and take tickets in their vintage uniforms. "They also sent out several members to play catch on the lawn before the show," Hoey says. "These guys would invite the patrons to join them, and many did." For *Over the River and Through the Woods,* the Italian-American Society came out to play bocce ball before the show; the Accordion Society of Central Illinois provided strolling musicians who played Italian folk songs for preshow entertainment. For *The Music Man,* barbershop quartets sang before the show.

"We offer these groups comp tickets for the performance," explains Hoey. "In most cases, they end up purchasing more tickets so their friends and family can come and see them. Hopefully, they enjoy themselves so much that they want to purchase season tickets, or come back for other specific shows. The purpose is twofold: first, provide a 'complete' evening of entertainment for our regular audiences, and second, introduce new people to The Tent."

When Okeechobee Community Theatre in Okeechobee, Florida, did *Steel Magnolias,* it gave buttons to local hairdressers. The buttons said "Ask me about *Steel Magnolias,*" and the hairdressers had tickets for sale in their salons. The theatre gave tickets and dinner to the hairdressers who sold the most.

The Actors Rural Theatre Company in Tuscola, Illinois, makes trips to county fairs in the region to sing portions of its current show.

The City Circle Acting Company in Coralville, Iowa, takes part in the annual Fourth of July parade with entries like skating nuns, who pass out fliers to the crowd.

On Halloween, Cedar Falls Community Theatre in Cedar Falls, Iowa, has the Phantom of the Opera outside at the marquee while trick-or-treaters go up and down Main Street.

Community Players, Inc., in Beatrice, Nebraska, served wedding cake following the opening night performance of *I Do! I Do!* A major college football team makes its home nearby, and on one game day, the theatre gave away door prizes to people who came to the show in team colors.

The point is, obviously, that the tie-ins are as endless as your shows. Each one offers your theatre different possibilities, unique to your community and your production. Take the time to look for ways to create extra fun, because it'll also create extra community awareness about your show . . . and more people are bound to check it out.

It's Not All Fun and Games

As fun as these ideas might be, don't expect any of them to cause a stampede to the ticket window. What they *will* do is enhance and supplement other aspects of your PR plan.

Gimmicks and publicity stunts provide additional opportunities for news coverage or fun feature-style photos. Does that directly translate into ticket sales? Maybe. But it certainly raises awareness about your theatre, and that's what good PR is supposed to do. Increased awareness over time does lead to increased ticket sales.

As for freebies and merchandise, you need to look at them as bonuses or rewards, not incentives. If someone is deciding whether to subscribe to your theatre's anniversary season, the deciding factor will not be whether she gets a lapel pin. But if she does subscribe, and does get a lapel pin, she'll think it's a nifty gift and will wear it around. Other people will ask, "Hey, where'd you get the nifty pin?" And that's when Jane Subscriber turns into a friendly mouthpiece for your theatre.

Take the Wilmington Drama League's magnets. "How successful were the magnets? I don't know," says managing director Ted Wilson. "I know a lot of people liked them, but I haven't followed up with giveaways since that first year and we keep growing."

In other words, the magnets were groovy but not essential. "I think giveaways like logo pencils, magnets, and the like are great as reinforcement pieces, but to me aren't the stuff that will ultimately sell tickets or garner more donations," Wilson says. "The magnets were one small element of a comprehensive marketing strategy that we developed to get our name out in public."

At this point, a little bell should go "ding" and a lightbulb should pop on over your head. Why? Because you just heard a very important idea: "a comprehensive marketing strategy." We'll talk more about that in the next chapter.

Better buckle your seat belt now.

A Request

If you have PR ideas you'd like to share for future editions of *The PR Bible for Community Theatres,* I'd love to see what you have. Write to me at

Jandoli School of Journalism and Mass Communication
Drawer J
St. Bonaventure University
St. Bonaventure, NY 14778
or email me at cmackows@sbu.edu

Things to Think About

- Which of these ideas appeals to you? Why?
- What giveaways could you afford?
- When and where could you give freebies away?
- What logo-adorned items could you sell?
- What sorts of tie-ins could you use to promote the shows in your next season?

16 Getting Your Act Together: Drafting Your PR and Marketing Plan

So here we are. Time to pull it all together. You need to have . . . *a plan.*

If you've skipped directly to this chapter hoping to get right to the good parts, or if you're in a bookstore trying to snatch nuggets of wisdom without actually buying the book, most of this isn't going to make sense without reading the previous fifteen chapters. Sorry. That's just how some books are, I guess. Go back and read the other stuff. The chapters are short, so at least it shouldn't take long. (If you're one of those bookstore readers, you're going to have to drink a lot of espresso so the manager doesn't boot you out or you're going to have to buy the book . . . buying the book will end up being cheaper.)

If you've done all your reading like you're supposed to, then you're ready to start planning.

There's No Business like Show Business . . . but There's No *Successful* Business like a Business that Uses PR Effectively

Why do you need a PR plan? Unfortunately, far too many theatres conduct their PR efforts on a show-to-show basis, where the season's

PR centers on the shows, or worse yet, a show-*by*-show basis, where there's no consideration of a season-long strategy at all. That approach is a survival mechanism, particularly for smaller theatres, but it's too short-sighted.

Instead, you want to shift your thinking so your PR efforts promote the theatre, not its shows. Yes, the shows make up the main portion of what the theatre does, but as the old adage goes, "There'll always be another show." In other words, shows come and go, but the theatre remains. So doesn't it make more sense to promote the theatre itself so it will *continue* to be around?

Don't misunderstand me. Promoting the theatre does not exclude you from promoting individual shows—but promoting shows often excludes you from effectively promoting the theatre. By getting too focused on the immediate project, you neglect to give appropriate attention and energy to the big picture. You miss the forest because you're looking at the trees.

Another problem with doing PR on a show-by-show basis, says Rod McCullough, managing director of the Fulton Opera House in Lancaster, Pennsylvania, is that you never present the theatre to the community as if it were an *entity* in the community. PR gives the theatre, as an entity, a face. McCullough uses the Fulton Opera House as an example. "It's important to us here that we are an arts resource to this community on and beyond the play that happens to be going on right now," he says. "We want people to know that no matter what play happens to be on the stage—whether they like that one or not—that's a different issue than whether there should be a Fulton Opera House."

You don't want people to think of your company as the group that did *My Fair Lady,* which they may or may not have liked; you want them to think of the theatre as a vital, integral community resource. *You want to create a sense that your community theatre belongs to the community.*

"Even more in a small community theatre that's volunteer driven, they need to create that vision, that mission, as to what it is their job is for that community and just say that over and over and over again," McCullough says.

For the Spirit of Broadway Theater in Norwich, Connecticut, that vision drives everything the theatre does, right down to the smallest of publicity efforts. "[We] make sure that the message in the sponsorship flyer is consistent with the message we have been promoting to the public," says CEO and artistic director Brett A. Bernardini. "We are engaged in using high-quality performing arts as the catalyst for the revitalization of our downtown and our communities in general," he explains. "It is that message we preach both to the public and to our business sponsors. We ask them to join our mission, *not* to donate money for a show. For us, the production is the vehicle by which we can make a lasting impact on our community, not simply produce a show and make money. It is a critical difference."

Strategy or Tragedy

McCullough and Bernardini both imply a familiarity and commitment to their theatres' overall vision and mission. Hopefully your theatre company has articulated its own vision and mission as part of an overarching strategic plan. Your PR planning needs to stem from that strategic plan.

If you don't have a strategic plan—something that will guide the theatre for the next three to five years (always keeping in mind that such plans have a degree of fluidity to them)—the theatre's board of directors needs to come up with one. A strategic plan says where the theatre wants to go; the PR plan, as a component of the strategic plan, serves as a vehicle to take it there.

Without a strategic plan, a theatre is like a ship without a rudder. Its sails—that is, the *sales* generated by PR and marketing—may move the ship along, but what's the purpose if the theatre doesn't know where it's going?

Take a look at the objectives and goals laid out in your theatre's strategic plan. As you craft a PR plan, make sure you address each of those goals and objectives—the PR plan should make some of them come to pass.

The PR Process

Now that you have some idea of what you want to say, you need to figure out how and why you're going to say it. For that, you need a little IROPEA (don't ask me how to pronounce that . . . I just made it up): identification, research, objectives, planning, execution, and assessment.

Identification

The first thing you need to do is identify your relationships. Remember all that time I spent in Chapters 2 and 3 talking about knowing your audiences and your media? Voila! Aside from your audiences and media, think of every other constituency you can possibly interact with: municipal governments, civic clubs, other arts groups, local restaurants, etc.

As you identify the theatre's relationships, evaluate them. Are things good? Pretty good? Good enough? Could they be better? Are the relationships beneficial or detrimental?

Research

Next, you need to have some information. To get it, you must conduct research about your theatre, your shows, your constituencies, and anything else you can think of that relates to the theatre. Don't overlook the small details, either. How many seats does your auditorium hold? How many of those seats can you actually sell? What are the time constraints of your volunteers? What building materials are available to you backstage or back at the warehouse?

When you're researching, it's always better to gather too much information than not enough. It will give you a better view of the big picture. The more information you have, the better decisions you'll make. You'll also have a better idea about how to best approach your constituencies.

Objectives

Your PR objectives should stem directly from the objectives in the theatre's strategic plan. They should all address the relationships between your theatre and its constituencies.

Objectives need to be specific and measurable. If they are, you'll know whether you achieved them. Seems simple enough, right? But in fact, objectives are one of the most problematic parts of the PR process.

"We're going to send out more newsletters this year" is *not* a good objective, even if it is something you want to do. It's not specific enough. When you say "more," do you mean an increased quantity of each issue? Of one issue in particular? Or do you plan to increase the frequency of the newsletter from four issues to six? How much does "more" even mean? A more specific objective would be, "We will increase our newsletter mailing list by 15 percent over the course of the season." That defines things better, and you can measure it.

Objectives get tricky because so much of what we do for PR is tough to measure. If you plan to "increase goodwill through our publicity efforts," how do you know you succeeded? Do you measure it by attendance? Donations? Subscriptions? Letters to the local newspaper saying how groovy you are?

On top of that, how do you identify whether one particular element of your plan is working or not? How do you know if, say, your bumper stickers have generated goodwill? Again, specificity and measurability are the keys. Find a way to measure goodwill in relation to bumper stickers. How about "We plan to generate goodwill by making free bumper stickers available to at least five hundred people." If people take the bumper stickers on their own from a table in the theatre lobby (as opposed to finding them stuffed in their programs), that's a good sign they *want* the bumper stickers, and that might be an appropriate way to measure goodwill.

Planning
Your plan is the specific steps necessary to carry out your objectives. We'll talk about the plan in more detail in just a bit.

Execution
By the time you execute your PR plan, you're carrying out a well-considered, well-researched timetable of actions aimed at achieving specific results. By this point, you're just following the schedule and making things happen.

Assessment
Once the PR plan is underway, you need to keep tabs on things to make sure it's working. You should continually assess and reassess the success of your strategies with one question in mind: Are you meeting your objectives? If you are, how does that fit within the overall strategic plan of the theatre? If you aren't, why not? What are the consequences, both for the theatre and for *you*?

Planning for the Plan

We've spent a few chapters looking at the relationships you need to *identify* and evaluate, and hopefully I've given you some ideas about what you should *research*. As far as *objectives,* you'll need to first look at your strategic objectives—something you have to do without me since they're specific to your own theatre.

Once that's all out of the way, you can start the *planning* process.

Your theatre's strategic plan is ideally a three- to five-year document that calls for some sort of growth or advancement. The PR plan will spur that growth in increments, so each PR plan should cover one year at a time. Take the approach, "Here's how this year's PR plan will forward the theatre's overall objectives." This allows you to keep focused on a manageable time period without getting *too* focused, and it also preserves the adaptability of the overall strategic plan. Then, when you start crafting your next PR plan, build on the growth achieved as a result of the first plan.

Remember, every part of your PR plan needs to work together to promote a consistent message, image, and look. Everything should also work together to promote the theatre and its activities, not simply the shows themselves.

Your plan should encompass the following:

- *Which mass media have you decided to use?* This should be based on research, not personal preferences.
- *Which controlled media are you going to use?* Use research to determine what has worked for you in the past. Then decide what, if anything, you want to try that's new.
- *Can you get a media sponsor?* If you reach an agreement with, say, a radio station, it's a professional courtesy to refrain from spending money with other stations. How will such an arrangement affect your use of other media outlets?
- *How much money will you spend on advertising?* Believe it or not, you may be able to get by without advertising. When I surveyed community theatres across the country, I discovered that around 33 percent of them did not buy any advertising in the mass media. Of those that did advertise, more than a third used only one media outlet. Not surprisingly, bigger theatres tend to spend more on advertising than smaller

theatres. Evaluate your own circumstances, but don't just assume you know what will work best.

- *When do your shows run?* The time of year can create certain challenges. For instance, have you ever noticed there's a lot of activity clutter in November and December? That makes it tougher to get your message out because so many other things are competing for your audience members' attention. But January and February are pretty quiet. Summer is hit-and-miss because so many people take vacations.
- *What nonshow events need publicizing?* Use those events to fill gaps between shows when your theatre might otherwise be dark.

The Plan! The Plan!

Your PR plan should be a master schedule of all the publicity- and marketing-related activities you'll conduct over the course of a season. Use specific dates for specific deadlines.

Let's start building a timetable.

PR for a Show

We'll begin with publicity for a single show. Get a calendar and pick one of your own shows and fill things in as we go. I usually work backwards from opening night of the run, but to avoid confusion, I'll go chronologically. Pick and choose what works for you from the list.

Two weeks before auditions:

- Send out a press release announcing auditions. Some theatres list audition dates for the season in their season brochures. Others put audition dates in the programs of preceding shows.

Two months before the show:

- Send out calendar listings to magazines and 'zines. Remember, some may require notice even further in advance. Some theatres prefer to see if they can cast a show before they send out any publicity.

- Plot out visits to civic and service organizations. The initial groundwork should be laid out months in advance; specifics need to be arranged as soon as casting is completed and cast availability determined.
- Arrange special publicity stunts.
- Arrange for theatre personnel to appear on radio and cable TV programs.

Following casting:

- Stress to the cast the importance of word of mouth. Ask them to talk the show up.
- Send out a press release announcing the cast members and where they're from. Highlight any previous experience any of them have with your theatre.
- Send out hometown press releases for any college students from out of town.

When people are measured for costumes:

- Take publicity mug shots to use in displays or publications. If you don't have costume measurements for the show, have photos taken within the first two weeks of rehearsal. That gives the photographer plenty of time to get the photos ready.

A month before the show:

- Send out PSAs to radio stations, the cable system's message channel, and the newspaper's calendar of events.

Three weeks before the show:

- Make arrangements with the newspaper for a review.
- Perform for civic groups and service organizations as their schedules allow during the next three weeks.
- Tape the cable TV show appearance (depending on the studio availability at the station).
- Take photos during rehearsal to use on sandwich boards or in displays.
- Remind your cast about the importance of word of mouth.

Two to two and a half weeks before the show:

- Start running your TV ads. Decide well ahead of time which channels and shows to advertise on.
- Mail your postcards.

Two weeks before the show:

- Hang your posters and fliers.
- Distribute table tents and placemats.
- Put up your sandwich boards.
- Mail your newsletters. If you send them bulk mail, do this a week and a half earlier.

Ten days to two weeks before the show:

- Send out a press release about the show that includes performance information, a show synopsis, and some comments from the director about the production.
- Start running ads in the newspaper. Run ads as your budget allows, but space them out so no more than three run per week. Aim for the Sunday lifestyles section if the paper has one. Ask about ad specials the paper may be running.
- Have cast members and the director appear on any radio talk shows you can schedule. If you have several shows, schedule them as close together as possible.
- Make public appearances and do publicity stunts.

One to two weeks before the show:

- Arrange for a feature story to appear in the newspaper. Aim for the front page of the Sunday lifestyle section if you can (but take what you can get). If possible, submit a photo or two to go with the story. Make sure you know if you're providing the story or if the paper is sending a reporter.
- Contact assignment editors in the news departments of local TV stations.
- Start running your radio spots. If you are able to do ticket giveaways, start the radio ads two weeks prior to opening, then scale them back when the ticket giveaways begin.

The week of the show:

- Run ticket giveaways on the radio.
- Arrange for guest appearances on a morning or afternoon radio

show on opening day or on the day or two before. It's also good to appear on radio during in-between weeks.

- Arrange to have a photo in the paper the morning of the show. If the local paper is a weekly, ask it to run a photo in the issue just prior to opening to preview the event, rather than in the issue after opening to report on the event.

If your show spans two or more weekends:

- Run radio spots during the in-between weeks. If you have a review you can refer to, make sure the spot plays up the show using the best comment or two from the review: "The *City Times* calls *Long Day's Journey into Night* one of the best plays of the year."

You may also want to allow for a review in there somewhere. Some newspaper reviewers come to dress rehearsal, some come to opening night, some come during opening weekend. Fill it in on your calendar, taking into account when the reviewer usually comes and how soon after the paper usually runs the review.

Within two weeks of closing, send out thank-you cards to everyone who participated in the show onstage, backstage, or in a support role. The board president or the entire board should sign them.

Within three weeks after closing, update the theatre's website.

Consider whether you are doing any special programming, like an author's talk or a public discussion about a play's social themes. Build in enough advance time to get arrangements set and special publicity for the event.

This is a crucial part of your PR plan: *Don't forget to build a production timetable for each of your printing jobs*—your posters, newsletters, postcards, fliers, programs, etc. Consult your printer about each project to come up with realistic dates. Add each production timetable to your master PR calendar.

Contributors to the newsletter should get to work on their articles as soon as a show is cast, and you need to make them stick to the deadlines you set as part of the PR schedule. Build in some leeway for yourself in case they don't make their deadlines.

Program info can sometimes be a last-minute thing, particularly for important things like "special thanks." Be aware of the need for flexibility when drafting the printing schedule for your programs.

PR for the Season

When you're done plotting out PR for the first show, do the same thing for your other shows. You'll get an idea of the PR overlap that may exist between them. That's good to know.

Looking at the season as a whole, what might make a good magazine story? You might not have a "wow" idea as part of the season. That's okay. Save your opportunity for when you really have something.

When does your annual meeting fall? Add to your PR plan the press release that announces the meeting. Nonprofits are also required to post a legal notice in the paper's classified section announcing the annual meeting—add that to the plan.

If you have any big announcements that will be made at the annual meeting, do a press advisory and invite the media. Prepare a press release to go along with the announcements, which can be sent out to media outlets that don't attend. Arrange for a photographer if you don't have someone who can take good pictures.

Issue a press release about the election of new board members and officers, providing a little biographical information about each.

When do you announce the next season? Add that press release to your calendar, then add a production timetable for that season's brochure. How does that tie in with or remain separate from events taking place as part of the current season?

Give your website an overhaul so it ties in with the season announcement.

PR for the Theatre

Now look at your PR plan. Are there any holes? When are there quiet times, when the public isn't hearing about the theatre for some reason? You need to fill those holes. You can do it with news about the theatre's annual fund-raiser. You can do it with news about the scholarship or public service award you present. You can do it with news about awards the theatre wins. You can do it with news about special events. (Heck, some theatres could fill one of those holes with a release about how they were featured in a book about PR for community theatres.)

You can also fill those holes by sending out your freebies, conducting your raffles, hosting special events, and holding play readings. Such events need publicity and they also create publicity.

The idea is to keep your theatre in the public's eye. That doesn't mean bash people with your presence . . . just give them reminders every so often that the theatre belongs to the community. PR is not about the shows, it's about the theatre's contributions to and involvement in the community.

That approach to PR also supports your theatre's other strategic goals. "We have a rather comprehensive follow-up for our sponsors," says The Spirit of Broadway's Brett Bernardini, "complete with marketing materials from the show, reviews, clippings, financial reports, photographs—everything and anything that will show the sponsor the impact their money made and how we affected a community with a production."

Finally, consider whether to publish an annual report. Such a report would recap the shows, provide financial information, offer an update on any special projects, and list all the donors. Include a message from the president addressing progress on meeting strategic goals. An annual report doesn't need to be big or elaborate, but make it as attractive as possible and make sure it's in keeping with the theatre's "look." The report's release should be timed to coincide with a gap in your PR plan *and* a major event like your annual meeting or donor reception or even fiscal year.

Tips for Execution

A good plan does you no good unless you execute it well. To do so,

- Execute the plan in a timely fashion. Get things to editors as quickly as possible. Build in enough lead time so you don't have to rush around at the end.
- Present yourself to the media in a professional but friendly manner. You know the old flies-with-honey adage.
- Prove yourself to be a trustworthy source of real information. Remember: No fluff.

Continuity is important for developing relationships. Assign certain tasks to specific people who can carry out those tasks over the long haul. This is particularly important for media relations and for working with a printer.

■ ■ ■

"I'm convinced that a large portion of marketing and PR is just being positive and being aggressive and being bright—constantly talking in a positive manner and getting other people to do the same."

Sam Kuba, executive director of Theatre Harrisburg (Pennsylvania)

■ ■ ■

Things to Think About

Haven't I given you enough to think about in this chapter already?

For More Information

If you need to tackle the strategic planning process, I suggest Twink Lynch's book *Boards in the Spotlight,* available from the American Association of Community Theatre. Lynch's book focuses on board development and responsibilities and how they tie into planning.

For more on PR and marketing, check out *Stage Directions Guide to Publicity,* edited by Steven Peithman and Neil Offen (1999, Portsmouth, NH: Heinemann).

Appendix

mitation may be the sincerest form of flattery, but it's also the best way to learn. This chapter offers a variety of examples you can follow, along with some explanations as to why they're put together the way they are. The examples are

1. a press release about a show
2. a press release for a news item
3. a press release about a person
4. a feature story release
5. a hometowner
6. a calendar listing
7. a fact sheet
8. a media advisory for a press conference or special event
9. a newsletter (two samples)
10. photographs

Make sure you look over all the examples. I included general tips wherever I could fit them, so there are nuggets of advice scattered throughout.

While the specific content of press releases will vary, the formula and format both remain pretty much the same. Don't look at these examples, then, and get caught up in the nitty-gritty of the content. Instead, look at how they're organized, look at what kind of information is presented and how it's presented, and look at the mechanics. If you do that, you'll be able to easily adapt these examples to fit your own needs.

Don't forget, practice makes perfect. The more press releases you write, the better you'll get. Keep at it, and you'll get to the point where you can write them in your sleep.

Some important things to remember when putting together a press release:

- Double-space.
- Use a one-inch margin all the way around.
- Use 12-point type in a serif font like Times, Times New Roman, or something similar. Fancy fonts are distracting and hard to read, especially in paragraphs. The same goes for sans serif fonts like Helvetica and Arial.
- Put your logo at the top. Also include the company's contact information, such as the mailing address, Web address, and phone number.
- Put *your* contact info (name, phone number, and even an email address) just above the headline. Make it easy for the editor to get in touch with you to answer questions.
- Leave a couple of inches of white space between your logo and the release information (the date, contact person, and contact person's phone number). This gives the editor room to jot notes when assigning your release to a reporter.
- Always end with your standard paragraph.
- End with "—30—" (but without the quotation marks) or three pound signs: ###. Those are both industry standards that indicate the release is finished.
- Always type the release. Hand-written releases are a no-no.

I have included a number of examples of standard paragraphs at the ends of the releases. They should give you a general idea of length and content.

The newsletter samples are intended only to show you basic design principles at work. I do not intend them to be *the* designs everyone should follow. The content of the newsletters is also intended to serve as models you can learn from, so don't forget to read the samples as well as the margin notes.

Finally, I'd like to thank Dick Marcott and Ardyth Van Scoy for their help with the photo samples. On each page, I suggest spots to crop the photos. Take a sheet of blank paper and place the edge where the arrow indicates and you'll see what the photo would look like cropped.

Example A–1

A press release about a show

Notice how
much lead time
this offers?

The logo is big and eye-catching.
Having the address next to it
makes the address easy to spot.

Albeeville Community Theatre
PO Box 007
Albeeville, NY 12345
www.albeeactors.com

Editors find it
helpful to have
space to jot
notes.

October 4, 2001   Contact: Chris Mackowski
For Immediate Release   (555) 555-1234

Albeeville Community Theatre to Perform *The Diary of Anne Frank*

The headline
should be in a
slightly bigger
font and in bold.

ALBEEVILLE, NY — Albeeville Community Theatre (ACT) will perform the wartime classic

The Diary of Anne Frank later this month.

Get the full
name in the
lead, followed by
an abbreviation.

Directed by William J. Smith, *Anne Frank* will be performed October 19-21 at Mt. Dew

University's Ibsen Arts Center. Friday and Saturday's performances will be at 7:30 p.m. and

Sunday's performance will be a 2:00 p.m. matinee. Tickets for *The Diary of Anne Frank* are

available at Poppy's, The Company Store, and the Ibsen Arts Center box office.

"*The Diary of Anne Frank* was a part of school curricula for two generations, so it's a story

familiar to many people," explains Smith.

The quotes
provide
information
rather than
fluff.

Anne Frank's plight was one true story out of more than 6 million: a Jewish family forced

into hiding to escape the terror of Nazism during World War Two. "Every day they lived in fear,"

explains Smith. "For two years, they woke up every day wondering 'This might be the day that

they find us.'"

In all, more than six million Jews, homosexuals, people with disabilities, and protesters were

put to death in German concentration camps.

(more)

If you're going to jump to
a second page, make sure
you let the editor know.
Don't assume an editor
will follow along.

Example A–1

A press release about a show (cont.)

Use a header to tie subsequent pages
back to page one. The blurbs should
be brief reminders of who the
release is from and what it's about.

ACT/*ANNE FRANK* (page 2 of 2)

"There are some people, particularly in today's younger generations, who don't know the

story. In many places, it's not even a part of the curriculum anymore," Smith says. "I have eleven-

and fourteen-year-old nephews who don't know this story," he admits.

A series of educational displays will be in the Ibsen Arts Center lobby. As part of the

performance, Smith has invited several students to read poetry written by children who had been

in concentration camps.

"If we forget this part of our history, it could recur in some fashion," says Smith. "We tend to

forget. It should be revisited many, many times."

Smith promises the show will be entertaining as well as educational, and he hopes audiences

also find it inspirational. "I don't want people to think, before they come see this show, that it's

going to be depressing," Smith says. "I want people to see this as hope. After all, that's what the

Franks had to live on."

Founded in 1979, Albeeville Community Theatre strives to stimulate and encourage interest

in the dramatic arts and enrich the community by providing opportunities for theatrical

involvement. A Company-in-Residence at Mt. Dew University's Ibsen Arts Center, ACT is

partially funded through a grant by the New York State Council on the Arts. Since its founding,

ACT has produced more than 60 shows.

—30—

This quote adds
an interesting
context to the
production.

If the editor
starts cutting
from the bottom,
nothing crucial
is lost.

An example of a
standard paragraph.

Don't forget to
let the editor
know you're
done.

Example A–2

A press release for a news item

Timeliness isn't as crucial for a
release like this. There's no
opening-night deadline.

Albeeville Community Theatre
PO Box 007
Albeeville, NY 12345
www.albeeactors.com

Give yourself
some space
between the
contact info, the
headline, and
the beginning of
the lead. The
white space
around the
headline will help
draw attention
to it.

April 9, 2001   Contact: Chris Mackowski
For Immediate Release   555-555-1234

Albeeville Community Theatre Honored for *Hello, Dolly!*

ALBEEVILLE, NY — Albeeville Community Theatre (ACT) has been honored by the

Theatre Association of New York State (TANYS) for its production last month of *Hello, Dolly!*

Three awards were given by TANYS adjudicator Mack Beth to the production, which ran

March 4-7, 2001, at the Marlowe Gardens Performance Center.

The first award, a Merit Award for Acting, was given to Joni Johnson of Albeeville for her

portrayal of Dolly Levi. "While Joni is no newcomer to ACT, this was her first leading role,"

said Mark Dribble, director of the production. "This is really a nice coup for her."

The director's
quotes offer
a bit of context
for each award
without sounding
self-congratulatory.

The second award, a Merit Award for Ensemble Work, was given to each member of the

Harmonia Gardens Wait Staff for their work during the number "Waiter's Gallop."

"The waiters had an incredibly complex choreography routine to pull off in that number, and

they did it in stunning fashion," said Dribble.

The final award, also a Merit Award for Ensemble Work, was given to the song and dance

team of Jeanne Hitchcock, Meredith VanDyne, Tommy Talltree, and Michael Mortimer. Mortimer

and Talltree played Cornelius Hackl and Barnaby Tucker, two men from Yonkers who've taken a

(more)

Example A–2

A press release for a news item (cont.)

The show's title is in italics, but the rest of the slug is unitalicized. The page numbers are italicized as well, but that's to set them off from the rest of the slug.

ACT/*DOLLY!* AWARD *(page 2 of 2)*

day off from work for a series of comical adventures in New York City, where they meet up with Hitchcock and VanDyne.

"This is the first time in ACT's history that specific groups of actors have been singled out from the larger cast and recognized for their work," said ACT President Darren Felshaw. "This was one of the most talented ensembles we've had on stage, so to have individuals singled out really speaks to the quality of their performances."

"I am very proud of all the award winners and know that all of ACT shares in their glow because, as always, it is a team effort that gets individuals such as these recognized," Dribble added.

Albeéville Community Theatre has offered local performers, technicians, and playwrights the opportunity to share their work with the community for twenty years. The company has won more than 30 awards from the Theatre Association of New York State, making it the most award-winning community theatre in the state. ACT always keeps its doors open to new, interested talent.

#

Your president is your theatre's figurehead and should *always* have something to say about important news.

Here, the director finally shows a little pride, but it's at the end, where the editor can chop it off if necessary.

An alternative format for ending a release.

Example A–3

A press release about a person

This is called a dateline. It does not have the date in it, but it does say where the story is happening.

If you're going to include the Web address, make sure the webpage is always up to date.

Albeeville Community Theatre
PO Box 007
Albeeville, NY 12345
www.albeeactors.com

November 13, 2000
For Immediate Release

Contact: Chris Mackowski
555-555-1212

It doesn't hurt to double-check your phone number. Did you notice this one was different?

Albeeville Community Theatre Hosts Playwright-in-Residence

ALBEEVILLE, NY—Albeeville Community Theatre (ACT) will host visiting playwright R.G. Rader early next month as part of the theatre's 4th season.

ACT will present a public staged reading of Rader's play *Heart-Beat* on Friday, December 1st starting at 7:30 p.m. at the Albeeville Public Library. Rader will be on hand to talk about the play with audience members. There will also be a wine-and-cheese reception.

If the editor cut out everything after the second paragraph, readers would still have the information they need to attend.

"We're pleased to continue our tradition of presenting original works," says ACT President Darren Felshaw. "A reading like this gives an author the chance to hear his play in front of an audience for one of the very first times. It's a helpful and essential part of the play development process. It isn't often that local audiences can participate in the creation of art like this, so it's really an exciting opportunity to see how a new play is shaped and developed."

Here's a great example of a quote used to educate the reader.

Heart-Beat tells a story of love found in one of the most unusual and haunting of places, the space between life and death in a coma. "These lost souls, trapped in limbo, must discover the true nature of love," says ACT Vice President Stan Stubinski, who will direct the reading. "For them, love really is a matter of life and death."

Admission to the reading is $1, although admission is free for ACT patrons. Tickets will be

(more)

The plot synopsis is short and sweet and tucked smoothly into the release. The quote from the director gives a hint of the play's mood and ambience.

Titles that precede a name are capitalized. Titles that follow a name are set off by commas and left lowercase: "...says Stan Stubinski, vice president of ACT, who will direct."

Example A-3

A press release about a person (cont.)

available at the door.

Also as part of Rader's visit, he will conduct a morning workshop with theatre students and creative writing students at the Albeeville Area High School. In the afternoon, he'll visit with students at Mt. Dew University.

In the spring, in cooperation with season sponsor WBLT radio, ACT will present Rader's *The Wind Behind Us*, a radio play that tells the heartwarming tale of an elderly couple who share a journey into town and into their past. Slated for production in Toronto in late 2001, Albeeville audiences will get to share in a sneak-preview of the script, performed by a local cast.

Rader divides his time between work as a professor, playwright, poet, and actor. He has had plays produced in New York City and New Jersey and has been writer-in-residence at the William Carlos Williams Center for the Arts. He is presently playwright-in-residence with Arrowhead Theater Company in New York City. In addition, he is the author of two books of poetry with his third collection to be published this winter. He holds degrees in philosophy, theology, and writing and lives with his wife, Mary-Jane, and son, Jason, in Passaic, New Jersey.

Now celebrating its fourth season, Albeeville Community Theatre seeks to promote, encourage, and produce community-based live theater in the greater Albeeville area. By making live theatre available and accessible to the public, ACT provides opportunities for community participation, appreciation and education, thus enriching the community and increasing interest in the arts.

— 30 —

Here's extra, related information in case the editor wants it—but it's not essential to the story. If you have the chance to smoothly plug an upcoming event, take it.

Always include some biographical information about the person. Work some of it into the release and save some for the end to act as a "standard paragraph" for the person. Follow it with your own standard paragraph.

When you send a release like this, it's usually helpful to have a photo of the person that you can send along with the release. Unless you specifically ask the paper to return the photo, they'll probably hang on to it.

Example A–4

A feature story release

Use the same format as you would for a regular news release.

For a feature story, it's okay to have the writer's byline appear if the writer wants credit for the story. Check with the editor to find out the newspaper's policy. Usually, the writer will get a credit like "By Chris Mackowski, Special to the Times Herald."

Albeeville Community Theatre
PO Box 007
Albeeville, NY 12345
www.albeeactors.com

You still need an angle for a feature, but you don't need an immediate hook. Features tell stories, so you can hook your reader by jumping right into the story. Then, unfold the angle over the course of a couple paragraphs. The angle here is the director's extensive experience and its effect on a new theatre group.

May 24, 2001
For Immediate Release

By Chris Mackowski
(555) 555-1234

Endwell Man Guides *Pippin* to the Stage for Albeeville Community Theatre

ALBEEVILLE, NY — "Let me see it again," says Mark Dribble as he crosses his arms and leans against the auditorium wall.

It'll be the third time through "Magic to Do," but the cast of *Pippin* laughs and chatters as they rise to their feet and prepare to run the dance routine one more time. Music director Andrew Alexander resets the computerized accompaniment, while choreographer Mary VanDyne takes a spot next to Dribble to watch her dancers.

It's a Tuesday night, a week and a half before the Albeeville Community Theatre (ACT) production opens, and spirits are high.

"This is ACT's first full-scale musical ever, so it's been quite a learning experience for them," says Dribble. "But the result is going to be an entertaining experience for the audience."

Dribble would know. In the more than two decades he's done theatre, this is his fourth time doing *Pippin*. Previously, he's directed the show twice and served once as a technical advisor.

"I'm amazed at the talent I'm working with here in Albeeville," Dribble says. "I'm working with the best dancer in the area, the best actor in the area, and some of the best vocalists I've ever worked with. This is undoubtedly the most experienced cast I've ever done this show with."

A few well-placed names can make people feel good. Alexander doesn't really play a part in this story, but since he's a major contributor to the show, it's nice to give him a mention as long as there's a smooth way to slip it in. It never hurts to boost morale! Likewise, mentioning VanDyne here lays the foundation for her appearance later in the article.

(more)

One of the main differences between a news release and a feature is that news releases get sent to all media outlets. With a feature release, send it to *one* paper only. It's a professional courtesy. Papers don't like to run feature stories their competitors also have. If you want a feature in more than one paper, write a different feature, with a different angle, for each paper.

Example A–4

A feature story release (cont.)

Sounds "political," doesn't it? Sure is!
This quote is not a happy accident—
it was a calculated PR move.

ACT/PIPPIN (page 2 of 4)

That experience, he says, has allowed him to explore the show on a deeper level than his

previous casts have been able to. "I haven't had to spend too much time on the basics this time

around," Dribble explains.

A resident of Endwell and a founder of Endwell Community Theatre (ECT), Dribble took on

the project in Albeeville because he was interested in helping ACT stretch its theatrical wings.

"I've been impressed by the dedication of the folks down here," Dribble says. "They're in their

fourth season, but what they may lack, as an organization, in theatrical knowledge, they make up

for in time, effort, and desire."

And that triumph of the human spirit is really what *Pippin* is all about. "The play shows how

indomitable the human spirit can be," Dribble explains. "Success comes with hard work."

* * * *

Dribble watches as the dancers go through their routine one more time. Pleased with the

result, he gives the nod, and VanDyne gives the dancers a short break.

Outside, it's raining. Still, a few cast members take a smoke break, huddled under the eaves

in front of Swarts Hall. Two of them run their dance moves.

Dribble comes out, carrying a one-liter bottle of Mountain Dew by its orange cap. "Nelson,

your turn with Mr. Churchill," he announces. The actor, Nelson Pauley, a veteran of ECT and

ACT shows, ducks back inside for his appointment with the music director.

"Nelson plays Charlemagne, Pippin's father," Dribble says. "He was in another show when

our rehearsals started and did a lot of schedule juggling so he could do this part. That's because,

for musical theatre folks, this is one of THE shows to do."

In fact, the cast consists of actors from as far away as Wellsville. Alexander, the music direc-

tor, commutes from Alfred. "There will be people who will rack up a thousand miles on their cars

commuting back and forth to rehearsals just so they can do this show," Dribble says.

That may seem odd for a show bereft of any readily-recognized songs—it has no musical

(more)

Here's a quote that ties the theme of the show together with the theme of the article. Again, not a coincidence; it's one of the reasons the writer chose this particular angle.

Indicate section breaks. With a long feature like this, a paper often breaks up the story to give the reader a spot to breathe. It's also a good place to shift the story's energy a bit.

Details help ground the reader in the present, and they can tell the reader a bit about the personality of the person in the feature.

Notice the pattern: the writer starts the article by grounding readers in a place and time, then goes off to explore the background info and quotes...then the writer brings the reader back to the present and moves the story along a little...then back to exploring...back to the present...back to exploring. By being grounded in the present, the reader has an easier time keeping track of what's going on.

Example A–4

A feature story release (cont.)

For people who don't know a particular show, a quote or two addressing that issue gives them a reason to come.

<u>ACT/PIPPIN (page 3 of 4)</u>

theatre standards like *Annie Get Your Gun* or *Gypsy* do. But Dribble says the show captivates performers and audience members alike. "It's such an up-tempo show," he says. "The songs aren't well-known, but the show still captures audiences' spirits and imaginations during the performance. Once people see it, they want to see it again and again and again."

The show is also popular among actors because of the strength of the chorus. "It's a troupe of actors telling the life story of Pippin, so the troupe really drives the story along. They provide the set-ups for the principal characters to tell their vignettes, so the troupe is integral to the show," Dribble says. "*Pippin* was really the first musical to feature the chorus as the driving force of the show."

Play up your people.

To bring the troupe to life, Dribble relied heavily on the choreography skills of VanDyne. Although she just finished her junior year at St. Bonaventure, VanDyne has the credentials of a salty veteran. She has choreographed for ECT and Kiwanis Kapers, and she has been honored by the Theatre Association of New York State (TANYS) with Merit Awards for her choreography, performing, and costuming.

She pops her head out the door to summon her last pair of dancers out of the rainy dusk: "C'mon, guys, let's get going."

* * * * *

Back inside, Dribble chats with Stephanie and Bob MacCleod, two of ACT's board members who are heading the show's tech crew. Both MacCleods are recent Simon University graduates, and recipient of the college's Robert C. Laing Creative Arts Award for Theatre. They studied under the same professor Dribble studied under more than twenty years ago.

Can the writer slip in a few more key people? Sure. But notice they actually relate to the "plot" of the feature story; they're not just tossed in because the writer wanted to stroke egos.

"It's wonderful to work with people who were trained by my mentor," Dribble says, speaking of the recently retired Dr. Patricia Bianco. "In a lot of ways, it's like coming back home to work on my home stage."

Dribble credits Bianco with laying the groundwork for his theatrical career. "In many ways,

(more)

Example A–4

A feature story release (cont.)

Remember to keep the header up-to-date.

ACT/PIPPIN (page 4 of 4)

she was a lot like my dad. She reinforced a lot of the same things: Do it right or don't do it."

Dribble has passed that philosophy on to the young people he now mentors, like VanDyne, vocal director Matthew Churchill, and a number of the cast members. "Knowing I serve to young people as the kind of mentor Patty was to me, even to a small degree, is the whole reason I do this," Dribble says. "It's the most rewarding part of theatre."

Warm and fuzzy is okay.

The MacCleods excuse themselves to go paint stained glass windows. Inside the auditorium VanDyne has started the dancers into their next routine.

Dribble smiles.

"Look at these people," he says. "Look at their enthusiasm. Look at their dedication. They're doing this RIGHT, or else we wouldn't be doing it. People are going to love this show."

The writer finishes where he started, providing a nice tie-up. He finishes with a feel-good quote—like a strong curtain line.

* * * * *

Albeeville Little Theatre presents *Pippin* in Simon University's O'Kain Auditorium

Thursday, May 31 at 7:30 p.m.

Friday, June 1 at 7:30 p.m.

Saturday, June 2 at 2:00 and 7:30 p.m.

Sunday, June 3 at 2:00 p.m.

Put your performance info at the end. Editors will often box it and use it as a sidebar to your story. With features, they don't chop from the bottom up, so you don't need to worry about losing it.

Tickets are available at The Gift Shop, Otto & Henry's Pharmacy, and Tina's Card Store. Pre-sale tickets are $6 and tickets at the door will be $7 for general admission and $6 for seniors and students.

Now celebrating its fourth season, Albeeville Community Theatre seeks to promote, encourage, and produce community-based live theater in the greater Albeeville area. By making live theatre available and accessible to the public, ACT provides opportunities for community participation, appreciation and education, thus enriching the community and increasing interest in the arts.

-- 30 --

Don't forget that standard paragraph, even on a feature release.

Example A–5

A hometowner

Albeeville Community Theatre
PO Box 007
Albeeville, NY 12345
www.albeeactors.com

Get that word "local" in the headline so editors know immediately why you're sending the release to them. Otherwise, they may wonder who you are and why you're sending them something—then pitch the release without reading it.

February 15, 2001
For Immediate Release

Contact: Chris Mackowski
(555) 555-1234

Local Student to Perform in *West Side Story*

ALBEEVILLE, NY — Albeeville Community Theatre (ACT) has announced the cast for its upcoming production of *West Side Story*.

Sylvia VanDyne, from Endwell, PA, will play the lead role of Maria. Sylvia is a junior communications major at Mt. Dew University. This is her third production with ACT.

Play up the featured person with some extra info.

West Side Story will be performed March 1, 2, 3, and 4 at the Albeeville Municipal Center's O' Kain Auditorium.

Founded in 1979, Albeeville Community Theatre strives to stimulate and encourage interest in the dramatic arts and enrich the community by providing opportunities for theatrical involvement. Since its founding, ACT has produced more than 60 shows.

—30—

What's of interest to the editor is the fact the student participated in the show, not the show itself. So, when mentioning the show, just stick with the basics.

Include your standard paragraph as a way to let the editor know who you are. They may use part of it if it will make the student look good.

Hometown releases can be a major inconvenience if you're sending them out two weeks before the show. Either send them early, like right after casting, or send them just after the show. It doesn't affect your audience either way since these aren't sent to local papers.

Example A–6

A calendar listing

Give yourself plenty
of lead time.

Albeeville Community Theatre
PO Box 007
Albeeville, NY 12345
www.albeeactors.com

February 9, 2001   Contact: Chris Mackowski
For Immediate Release   (555) 555-1234

This is not
intended as a
release, so you
need to specify
that to the
editor.

Calendar Listing

Editors: Please include the following in your calendar of events.

Boil everything
down to the bare
essentials: who,
what, when, where,
and how much.

Albeeville Community Theatre will present William Shakespeare's *The Tempest* on
March 9 and 10, 2001, at 7:30 p.m. in the Albeeville Municipal Center's O'Kain
Auditorium. Admission is $6 at the door.

Different time,
different listing.

Albeeville Community Theatre will present William Shakespeare's *The Tempest* on
March 11, 2001, at 2:00 p.m. in the Albeeville Municipal Center's O'Kain Auditorium.
Admission is $6 at the door.

— 30 —

Example A–7

A fact sheet

Albeeville Community Theatre
PO Box 007
Albeeville, NY 12345
www.albeeactors.com

A Biography of Albeeville Community Theatre (ACT)

Albeeville Community Theatre seeks to promote, encourage, and produce community-based live ◄—— — Recognize this?
theater in the greater Albeeville area. By making live theatre available and accessible to the
public, ACT provides opportunities for community participation, appreciation and education,
thus enriching the community and increasing interest in the arts.

ACT was founded in the fall of 1996. Our first production, *The Foreigner*, was mounted in the
spring of 1997. We are currently in the midst of our fourth season, and plans are underway for our
fifth anniversary season.

The current president of ACT's board of directors is Darren Felshaw.
The other board members are: ◄——————
    Archie Cunningham (secretary)
    Mark Dribble
    George Edinboro
    Margaret Kallakowski (vice president for membership)
    Betsy Marsh (treasurer)
    Bob O'Donnell
    Stephanie Seymour
    Stan Stubinski (vice president for artistic direction)

— A community
theatre's
greatest asset is
its people.
Highlight them.
Use their names
whenever possible
when dealing with
the local media.

ACT is a member of the American Association of Community Theatre (AACT) and the Theatre
Association of New York State (TANYS). ACT is also signing on as a charter member of the new
Twin Tiers Arts Alliance (TTAA), a consortium of arts groups in rural southwestern New York
and northwestern Pennsylvania.

(more)

Example A–7

A fact sheet (cont.)

This might be impractical if you're an older group. Hit the most successful highlights.

ACT FACT SHEET *(page 2 of 2)*

A list of ACT's productions to date:
The Foreigner by Larry Shue — May 1997
A Coupla White Chicks Sitting Around Talking by John Ford Noonan — August 1997
Lies & Pizza (co-sponsored with Mt. Dew University's Theatre Department) — March & April 1998
Steel Magnolias by Robert Harling — May 1998
Summer's Way by Chris Mackowski (co-sponsored with Endwell Little Theatre) — July & Aug. 1998
The Fantasticks (Albeeville's first community musical in eight years) — Sept. 1998
The Glass Menagerie by Tennessee Williams — February 1999
The Odd Couple by Neil Simon (the female version) — May 1999
That's Absurd, A Collection of Stories and Surprises from the Theatre of the Absurd (featuring *Breath and Krapp's Last Tape* by Samuel Beckett, *The Zoo Story* by Edward Albee and the original works *Illumination* by Stan Stubinski and *Toast* by Amy Godfrey) — June 2000
How I Learned to Bellydance by Chris Mackowski — September 2000
Emma's Child by Kristine Thatcher — February 2001

Highlight anything unusual or innovative your group does.

Our playwright-in-residence series, started in our third season, has featured staged readings of new works with post-reading Q&A sessions, meet-the-author receptions, and classroom visits to schools.
1999-2000 Katt Lissard *Excavation*
2000-2001 R.G. Rader *Heart-Beat* and *The Wind Behind Us* (a radio play forthcoming on WKWK radio this spring)

What makes your group unique?

We have mounted productions of four original plays in our first four seasons, making us the region's leader in promoting new work by local playwrights.
· *Summer's Way* by Chris Mackowski, which toured seven communities in five counties and two states
· *Illumination* by Stan Stubinski
· *Toast* by Amy Godfrey of Olean, NY
· *How I Learned to Bellydance* by Chris Mackowski, which earned two Merit Awards from the Theatre Association of New York State
Additionally, we co-sponsored *Lies and Pizza* with Mt. Dew University's Theatre Department. The production consisted of four staged readings of original plays by local playwrights.

Play up local angles.

Awards always look nice.

Example A–8

A media advisory for a press conference or special event

Give editors enough of a heads-up, but not so
much lead time that they spill the beans too soon.
If it's a good story, a reporter isn't going to want
to sit on it too long.

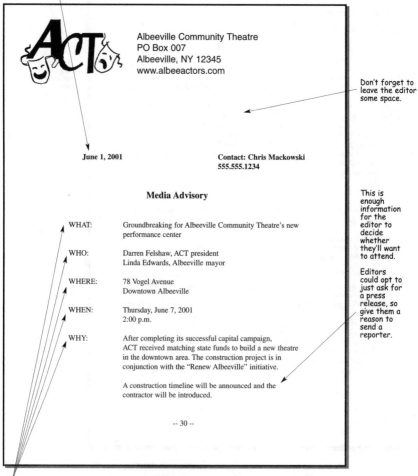

Albeeville Community Theatre
PO Box 007
Albeeville, NY 12345
www.albeeactors.com

Don't forget to
leave the editor
some space.

June 1, 2001   Contact: Chris Mackowski
                                555.555.1234

Media Advisory

WHAT: Groundbreaking for Albeeville Community Theatre's new
          performance center

WHO: Darren Felshaw, ACT president
          Linda Edwards, Albeeville mayor

WHERE: 78 Vogel Avenue
          Downtown Albeeville

WHEN: Thursday, June 7, 2001
          2:00 p.m.

WHY: After completing its successful capital campaign,
          ACT received matching state funds to build a new theatre
          in the downtown area. The construction project is in
          conjunction with the "Renew Albeeville" initiative.

          A construction timeline will be announced and the
          contractor will be introduced.

-- 30 --

This is
enough
information
for the
editor to
decide
whether
they'll want
to attend.

Editors
could opt to
just ask for
a press
release, so
give them a
reason to
send a
reporter.

Just the
facts, ma'am.
Just the
facts.

When you send an advisory, ALWAYS follow up to make
sure the editor got it. It's also helpful, for planning
purposes, to check the day before the event to see if
the editor is sending anyone to cover it.

Example A–9

Newsletters (Sample I, page I of 4)

See the strong visual lines that exist here in the corner even without actual lines on the page? That helps keep a publication unified and it guides the eye.

If you're going to break a visual line, do it on purpose, for intentional effect, not by accident. It can make your newsletter look sloppy.

Show titles can be turned into art and used with other artwork (as is done here) or used independently as a graphic element in other forms of PR, in essence acting as a logo for the show.

What sort of "look" does this font create? You'll see a number of ways the design reinforces that look throughout the newsletter.

The designer chose to align the As, as well as the vertical lines in the I and the L.

June '00
vol. 4
ish. 3

Albeeville Community Theatre · PO Box 007 · Albeeville, NY 12345 · www.albeeactors.com

ACT About to Get "Absurd"

"Only $1 for an evening of theatre?" you ask?
"That's absurd!" you say?
Exactly!
Albeeville Community Theatre (ACT) is getting ready to get absurd, and you're invited.
ACT presents *That's Absurd!*, an evening of stories and surprises from the Theatre of the Absurd, June 23-25, 2000, at 7:30 p.m. nightly in Simon University's O'Kain Auditorium. Admission is only $1.
Yep. A buck.
"We're trying something new this year," says ACT President Darren Felshaw. "We call it our Summer Buck Show. The idea is to present something 'different' than the type of theatrical experience most of us are used to."
"Different" may only begin to describe the line-up of shows in *That's Absurd!*, although "challenging and fun" would also be appropriate.
The evening starts with a short play by Samuel Beckett called *Breath*. "I love this show because it challenges every single notion people have about the definition of 'theatre,'" says director Stan Stubinski. "People may see it and actually wonder 'That was a play?'"
While that might not sound like a ringing endorsement to get audience members flocking to the door, Felshaw promises people won't be disappointed. "I was unfamiliar with some of these plays, and after having watched them, I found them to be a lot of fun," he says.
A second Beckett show, *Krapp's Last Tape*, is also on the docket for the evening. The play stars ACT veteran Dick Marriott as Krapp, a man who spends his birthday listening to tape recordings he's made on previous birthdays. The result is the older, cynical Krapp engaged in a conversation with his younger, idealistic self. "Hindsight is always twenty-twenty," says Marriott. "Krapp listens to the tapes of his past because that's all he has. He's so disappointed in the present that he can't face it, but that's the irony. If he faced the present, he might have more than his tapes." see "Absurd" on page 2

Be careful you don't "trap" odd-shaped white spaces, which can unintentionally make a piece look choppy.

Just a side note: *Curtain Call* is far and away the most popular theatre newsletter name. Of all the samples folks sent me, more than half were named *Curtain Call*. Great minds think alike!

The double lines tie into the masthead font and the double lines that surround the contact info. Continue to use the double lines as a graphic element that runs elsewhere, creating a sense of unity throughout the newsletter.

This is the same font as the headline, reinforcing the sense of unity throughout the publication.

Example A–9

Newsletters (Sample I, page 2 of 4)

The bottom of the page number aligns with the bottom line, reinforcing the visual lines.

As a regular newsletter feature, you can put the title in the same font as the masthead, which increases the column's importance.

The photo's border is the same width as the other lines, adding to the sense of consistency.

2

COMPANY NEWS

❧Congratulations to former board of directors member Angela Asako on her recent engagement. The happy couple will tie the knot this October, and they'll make their home in Chicago.

We like to think we aren't really losing a director...we're gaining a son.

❧Kudos to ACT VP Stan Stubinski, who graduated earlier this month with a Master of Fine Arts degree in creative writing from Goddard College.

This may come as a shock to folks, but Stan concentrated in playwriting. Stan has written four plays produced by ACT, including last year's *Endwell*.

❧ACT passes our condolences on to the family of Vinay Naryanan, who passed away last April after a struggle with cancer.

Vinay appeared in ACT's 1998 production of Terrence McNally's *A Perfect Ganesh* as the Indian god Ganesha. His performance netted him a TANYS award.

❧If you missed ACT's radio production of *The Wind Behind Us* last month, you'll soon have the chance to tune in again. The show was such a success that a rebroadcast will air on WESB on the Fourth of July at 9:00 p.m.

The Wind Behind Us, by ACT's 1999 Playwright-in-Residence, R.G. Rader, tells the story of an elderly couple who, during a walk into town, have the chance to revisit their past.

That's Absurd! full of surprises con't. from page 1

Krapp is also directed by Stubinski, who admits he's a big fan of playwright Beckett. "Hands down, he's the most influential playwright of the twentieth century. It's exciting that we're able to bring some of his work to life for folks here in Albeeville," Stubinski says.

The evening also includes an Absurdist play by local playwright Chris Mackowski called *Illumination*. "It's a play about a lightbulb," says Mackowski. "I can't tell you much more than that because I still haven't figured it out for myself," he laughs.

Topping off the evening is *The Zoo Story* by Edward Albee, directed by Mark Dribble. An encounter between two men in New York's Central Park turns both of their lives upside down.

"We all have those things that come out of left field and hit us right between the eyes and shake us down to our toes," says Dribble. "Sometimes it's tough to make sense of those things, no matter how much we struggle with them."

The Zoo Story features Moe Stevens and Matthew Churchill. This is Stevens's first appearance with ACT, although he recently appeared as Daddy Warbucks for Endwell Little Theatre. Churchill last performed for ACT in last year's award-winning production of *Picnic*.

Felshaw also says audience members should expect the unexpected. "We've got some extra treats in store," he promises. "I think people will be delighted by the surprises they encounter."

And at a dollar a ticket, Felshaw is sure people will get more than their money's worth.

"We felt it was important, as part of educational mission, to present our audience members with something that stretches their theatrical experiences a bit," Felshaw says. "We've done Simon and Shakespeare and Miller. We felt it was time to push the boundaries a bit." ❧

Matthew Churchill (standing) and Moe Stevens are headed toward a crash-course collision in Edward Albee's *The Zoo Story*, part of ACT's Summer Buck Show *That's Absurd!*

This picture would be better if we could see the knife more clearly. But notice how the shadows in the lower-right corner add to the sense of creepiness?

The caption font matches the headline font, adding to the sense of unity throughout.

Here's another way to use the double lines as a visual element.

A dingbat at the end of an article serves as a visual cue that the article is over. Depending on the dingbat you choose or create, it can also serve as a visual element that ties back to your logo somehow. You can also use variations of the dingbat as a design element elsewhere.

A regular feature like this column builds a sense of family for volunteers and participants, and it creates a sense of familiarity for readers. Notice the use of first, rather than last, names, and the more informal style? It helps people get invested in your theatre because it puts a human face on things.

A box helps organize what might otherwise look like a bunch of free-floating blurbs.

It might be tempting to leave a space like this empty. Don't. It looks bad, and it's a wasted opportunity to say something. How about another quote from someone? What about enlarging the picture slightly?

Example A–9

Newsletters (Sample 1, page 3 of 4)

The president addresses an audience concern. The president should always discuss a "big picture" issue and not get bogged down in simple cheerleading for shows (although cheerleading is important, too).

The font for the page number matches the masthead font. But notice the designer hasn't gone "font crazy." Three fonts only: Times for article text, Helvetica for headlines and captions, and Delphian for standard newsletter features.

Your president is a figurehead, so make him visible and recognizable. A mug shot with his column is a MUST.

3

Summer Buck Show the latest offering in an exciting season

You wanted summer theatre—you got it!

What a sensational year this has been for ACT.

If you've been to the shows this season, you know what I'm talking about. If you haven't, there's still time to join the fun and excitement.

As you've no doubt read already, ACT is launching what we hope will become a summer tradition: ACT's "Summer Buck Show." The idea is to present something a little different than our usual fare. It's a chance for us to find small pieces that might be a bit unconventional so we can stretch your imaginations—and ours.

We've had a lot of requests over the past few years for some sort of summer offering, but because of vacation schedules we've found it challenging to mount anything. The board has wracked our collective brains for a solution and—we're pretty excited about what we came up with. We think this will fit the bill perfectly.

It's a chance for us to... stretch your imaginations— and ours.

FROM THE PRESIDENT

To make the experience as inviting as possible, we're only charging a $1 admission fee. That serves two purposes: first, it keeps the "risk" down for those of you who might not be sure what you're getting yourselves into. It also makes it possible for anyone and everyone who wants to enjoy live, community-based theatre to come and enjoy a show.

Of course, at a buck a ticket, we'd have to sell a lot of tickets to meet our costs. Fortunately, City Bank has joined us to help bring our Summer Buck Show to you. We also want to extend our thanks to media sponsor WWIT-FM for their help in promoting the show.

I'm also pleased to report that our production of *The Island of Dr. Moreau*, written by our own Chris Mackowski, won a pair of Merit Awards from the Theatre Association of New York State. The show set a box-office record for us for the largest opening-night attendance for a straight drama. We thought that was sensational enough, but with these two awards added on top of that, we're bursting at the seams.

Our season wraps up in August with *Emma's Child*, and then we'll be ready to launch another season of excitement soon thereafter. If you think this season has been sensational (we sure do), wait'll you see what we have in store. Watch out for details!

Until then, I'll see you at the theatre!

Darren Felshaw
Darren Felshaw,
President, ACT

If you don't have a photo to go with a large article, you can use text as a visual element to break up the page. Notice, this font matches the headline and caption font. It's yet one more place to use repetition to build unity.

A signature always makes the president's column look more official and personal.

Moreau wins awards for set, lights, make-up

The Theatre Association of New York State (TANYS) has recognized ACT's recent production of *The Island of Dr. Moreau* with two awards.

The first Merit Award went to set designer Jon Longfellow and lighting designer Mark Dribble for the stage environment they created. "I was astounded at the way in which the set and the lights worked together to create such a wondrous sense of space," said adjudicator Ruth Pwilger. "It was beautiful to look at and experience."

Pwilger also recognized make-up designer Pauline Fiennes with a merit Award. "The make-up really underscored the whole idea that these creatures were less-than-human," the adjudicator said.

Moreau director George Wells lauded his designers for their work. "ACT has some of the best designers in the state working with us," he said. "They did such an outstanding job creating a believable world for this story about unbelievable things."

Congratulations to all three Merit Award winners!

Steffie Stubinski was one of twenty Beast People make-up artist Pauline Fiennes created for every performance.

Photos are a subtle way to reinforce your values and mission. For instance, if you promote yourself as a family theatre, tossing in a picture of a young actor once in a while reminds everyone that you have a theatre for all ages.

The bottom of the article should line up with the bottom of the caption. Otherwise, there's no visual bottom to the page.

Where are your double lines? If you establish a design rule, such as "lines beneath a caption," you need to stick with it.

Example A–9

Newsletters (Sample 1, page 4 of 4)

Mr. & Mrs. Theatre Patron
25 Elm Street
Albeeville, NY 12345

Don't miss our next show:
That's Absurd!
June 23-25, 2000

Here's a chance to get in an extra plug.

Albeeville Community Theatre
PO Box 007 · Albeeville, NY 12345
www.albeeactors.com

The post office won't deliver without proper postage!

Don't violate the fold by running over. Doing so looks sloppy.

Build in a little extra space in case the newsletter gets folded unevenly.

fold line

4

Coming this August from ACT...
A tale of heartbreak and hope....

Emma's Child

ACT's season wraps up in August with *Emma's Child*, directed by Fumiko Murakami.

"*Emma's Child* touches the human spirit and asks all of us to consider what we would do or could do when life deals us less-than-ideal circumstances…when we face challenges in our lives that seem almost too much with which to cope," says Murakami. "It asks us to consider what we know about ourselves and our loved ones."

Jean and Henry Farrell, played by BLT veterans Sharie Buckingham and Mick Cousins, want to adopt a baby and bring a new and exciting dimension to their relationship. But when the child is born with severe health problems, Henry changes his mind—but Jean falls in love with the baby, and the attention she gives the child threatens her marriage. Meanwhile, the birth mother vanishes before Jean's parental rights are finalized.

Can Jean and Henry find solutions to the differences they learn about each other, or is their relationship doomed because of the events and problems surrounding the birth of this child?

Emma's Child runs August 11 and 12, and again August 18 and 19, at 7:30 p.m. in the O'Kain Auditorium at Simon University. ACT will present 2:00 p.m. matinees on Sunday, August 13 and 20.

Rounding out the cast are Mo Hammersmith, Jake Augustini, Suzie Schwartz, Leslie Boser, Michelle Michaels, Gay-Yee Summers, Karen Zremski, and Jamal Andrews.

Here's a good place to show off the artwork for the next show. This artwork should have already appeared in the season brochure, so this is merely a reintroduction.

If the newsletter is folded, people can still see a logo.

This is a high-profile spot because it's on the outside when the newsletter is folded and tabbed.

Example A–9

Newsletters (Sample 2, front page only)

Look at the strong line that runs down the right side of the shaded box. The intent is to guide the reader's eye downward rather than let it wander elsewhere on the page.

What effect is created by violating this strong border with the photo? Doesn't it make the picture stand out more?

What sort of look does this font create? Notice this sample has only two fonts: Times for the text and Onyx for the headlines and captions.

Another example of artwork for a show title.

Here, the president's column has a photo to go with it. The column has also been placed in a prominent position.

The lines on this page are very strong and straight, yet this element is curved. The contrast draws attention to it.

Nov '00
vol. 4
ish 2

Albeeville *Community* Theatre
PO Box 007
Albeeville, NY 12345
www.albeeactors.com

Playwriting a Breeze for *Wind* Author

ACT's Visiting Playwright Encourages Audiences to Explore "the Quiet Places"

A Happy ACT Anniversary from Us to You

Five years ago, a group of people sat around a dining room table in a home on Stone Avenue and decided to bring community theatre back to Albeeville.

It had been 20 years since the dissolution of the Highland Players. In the interim, ACPAC had presented large-scale community musicals; the ever-present Kiwanis Kapers offered plenty of laughs; and even Albeeville-U's student productions offered an occasional spot for a community member or two. But, for the most part, the niche left by the HP remained unfilled.

ACT would change that. It would bring live, community-based theatre back to Albeeville. Residents would once again have a theatre they could call their own. I, for one, was excited. Everyone around that table shared that excitement.

Now, five years later, we're more excited than ever.

Last season was a big turning point for
... continued on page three
... see "President"

ACT President
Darren Felshaw

The Wind Behind Us

Mo Hammersmith and Karen Zremski star in the premiere of *The Wind Behind Us*, a radio play by playwright-in-residence R.G. Rader, December 1, 2000, at 7:30 p.m.

Playwright R.G. Rader has spent his writing career thus far taking his characters, and his audiences, into "the quiet places." Fitting, then, that he escapes the hustle and bustle of New York City during this first week of the holiday shopping season to come to Albeeville for the staged reading of his newest work, *The Wind Behind Us*.

"It's important to get out of the city once in a while," he laughs. "Particularly at this time of year!"

Rader will be on hand for the reading, which will be held on Friday, December 1 at 7:30 p.m. in the Albeeville Area Public Library. The reading will also be simulcast on WWIT-FM radio. Admission to the reading is $1 for the general public and free for ACT subscribers. A reception will follow.

Also following the reading, Rader will take questions and gather feedback from the audience about the play. "I'm very interested in hearing what people have to say about my work," he says. "Everything sounds perfect in my head while I'm writing it, but I can't really tell if they work until I hear those words come out of the mouths of actors and I hear where and how the audience responds."

The Wind Behind Us is about an elderly married couple who are taking a walk into town. "The couple has a few unexplainable experiences along the way," Rader says. "They eventually realize they're not just walking to town, they're walking back into their youth. They have the chance to relive life."

The play, then, he says, "is about finding love, honesty, sincerity, and especially fulfillment even in the good times and the bad."

Rader says the focus of much of his work aims at getting into the silent places where we do our own reflecting. "I like to find ways to get to places where we, as individuals, don't allow others, or if we do allow others, we need to trust them very much," Rader explains. Those spaces exist, he says, "in the depths of our thought, in memory, in places where we go internally, dealing with our soul and our faith. I look for
... continued on page two
... see "Wind"

www.albeeactors.com

Avoid crowding text against the edge of a box. Give yourself some breathing room. This is about the minimum.

The shaded box creates contrast between sections of the page.

Here's a chance to not only slip in your Web address again, but also provide a tidy visual wrap-up to the page.

Did you notice this newsletter has no title? If you didn't notice, why not? Could it be because there's so much else at the top to look at?

Example A–10

Photographs

This photo was taken from straight on, about two and a half feet in front of the actor.

Dick insisted he was smiling in this picture. Often, actors think they're smiling, but their smiles aren't big enough to "play" on camera.

This photo was taken from straight on but slightly stooped, about two and a half feet in front of the actor.

You may need to get your subject warmed up a little so he doesn't feel self-conscious about getting his photo taken.

Be conscious of your subject's posture. Dick looks stiff in the left picture; he looks much more relaxed in the right.

Left, Dick is standing ramrod straight and pointed directly at the camera. Right, he's seated on a stool, leaning his arm slightly on his downstage leg. He's also facing down-left a bit. This creates angles on two different axes, which gives the photo depth.

Watch out for glare on glasses! Many a groovy photo has been wrecked by glare.

This photo was taken from straight on, about three feet in front of the actor.

Crop a little off the back since it's all dead space.

This photo was taken from the house floor, down-right of the actor, who was standing on a piano stool.

Speaking of posture, can you tell Ardyth is a dancer?

Her arms and face, because they're light, stand out against the darker background. Her pose is interesting because we can see the unusual positioning of her arms so well. But notice that her dark shoes are lost against the dark floor.

If we shift the angle, as we do in the right photo, we can better see her entire body's positioning. She also seems a bit larger than life because we're shooting from a low angle, which makes a subject seem bigger or more powerful.

Ardyth looks like she's ready for some Kung-Fu fighting in the left photo, but she looks like a Grecian statue in the right.

Example A–10

Photographs (cont.)

This photo was taken from just off the edge of the stage, slightly toward house-right.

Look at that vast empty space between Ardyth and Dick. Your eye ping-pongs back and forth between them because there's no obvious element commanding attention.

There's also a lot of space behind Ardyth, which makes it seem like she's just floating around out there. Try cropping at the arrow and see if that grounds her a bit more.

Dick's face competes with his shorts for attention because they're both light areas set against darker backgrounds. His shorts are bigger, and his bare legs add to the light area, so guess what wins?

This photo was taken on the stage, about three feet in front of and slightly downstage from the actor in the foreground.

By switching angles, you can eliminate the empty space. Notice how that creates a stronger relationship between the actors. And doesn't it now seem like something's actually happening in the picture?

Dick's face also gets more emphasis. It isn't competing with his shorts anymore, and we're close enough to get a better view of his expression. With his dark shirt acting as a background, his crossed arms also get a lot of emphasis, which adds to the emotional content of the photo.

Ardyth's face gets emphasized, too. Although she's in the background, her light face stands out against the dark background.

Example A–10

Photographs (cont.)

This photo was taken from the house floor at center stage.

Dick may have cute legs, but they detract from the photo. After all, what's important here? The box, right? But the box is so small that it's really lost in the middle of the picture.

All the curtain space around the two actors pulls our attention away from the important part of the picture, too.

Nothing under the table adds to the telling of the story in the picture, either. It's clutter.

Dick and Ardyth have nice reactions to whatever they've found in the box, but the picture was taken from too far away to highlight their facial expressions.

This photo was taken on the stage, about three feet in front of and slightly downstage from the actors.

Get closer! By moving in, we eliminate a lot of the empty space around the actors (although we could still crop some out of the left side of the picture). We also lose the clutter of legs under the table.

It's much easier to focus on the box and the faces. The dark clothes create good contrast for the light faces, and we're now close enough to get a great look.

We've also added levels to the photo by having Ardyth stand. Ask any good director and she'll tell you levels are good because they improve the stage picture. The same goes for pictures you take on stage.

AM7067-2
9   CA